GRADES 3-8

HOW TO CREATE A COLLEGE DAY

☆ AND ☆

OTHER COLLEGE READINESS ACTIVITIES

BY LISA KING, ED.S

youth light
inc.

© 2015 YouthLight, Inc.
Chapin, SC 29036

All rights reserved.
Permission is given for individuals to reproduce the activities and worksheet sections in this book.
Reproduction of any other material is strictly prohibited.

Design by Melody Taylor
Project Editing by Susan Bowman

ISBN: 978-1-59850-174-2
Library of Congress Number: 2015933810

10 9 8 7 6 5 4 3 2 1
Printed in the United States

BOOK INCLUDES:

Step by Step Guide and Timeline for Creating a College Day · PowerPoints to Teach Lessons · Word Puzzles, Crosswords
Templates for Letter/Forms for College Day · Articles about Different Aspects of Post High School Options
Bulletin Board/Door Decorating Ideas · Craft Ideas and Lesson Plans

TABLE OF CONTENTS

SYNOPSIS

School counselors often focus on teaching career awareness, but what about the training prior to a career? How about establishing a College Day!? This idea can be tweaked in many ways to suit the needs of your school. Discover a variety of activities to help you create a College Day or even a College Week. Kids of all ages love to learn about the possibilities ahead of them whether it is vocational school or a four-year university. This book will walk you through creating a round-robin of speakers, implementing lessons, providing supplemental worksheets and many other activities to explore post high school education. As educators, we know that "students with an eye on the future, do better in the present." What better way to get them excited for the future than to hear about all of the options.

Book includes:
- Step by Step Guide and Timeline for Creating a College Day
- Templates for Letter/Forms for College Day
- PowerPoints to teach lessons
- Word Puzzles, Crosswords
- Bulletin Board/Door Decorating Ideas
- Brief Articles written about different aspects of post high school options
- Craft Ideas
- Lesson Plans

WHY COLLEGE READINESS FOR YOUNGER STUDENTS?

"If we don't put the idea of college on the table early, the likelihood that kids are going to go to college is very low. It has to be part of their dream; you have to ingrain it in their plan for the future." —Marta Tienda, Sociologist, Princeton University

The College Board's National Office for School Counselor Advocacy is an organization that "identifies and supports the skills, practices, characteristics and relationships for school counselors necessary to ensure that all students are college-and-career-ready." NOSCA puts into perspective an important framework for elementary and middle school students. It reiterates the basis for this book and the need for curriculum aimed to this age group for college readiness skills and moreover a college going mentality.

Eight Components of College and Career Readiness	Are these components taught in		
	Elementary	Middle	High
College Aspirations	yes	yes	yes
Academic Planning for College and Career Readiness	yes	yes	yes
Enrichment and Extracurricular Engagement	yes	yes	yes
College and Career Exploration and Selection Process	yes	yes	yes
College and Career Assessments	yes	yes	yes
College Affordability Planning	yes	yes	yes
College and Career Admission Processes	no	no	yes
Transition from High School to College Enrollment	no	no	yes

http://nosca.collegeboard.org/

HOW TO USE THIS BOOK

If your school wants to implement a theme of College Readiness, this book will help establish these ideas that could be introduced from a one day College Day to a yearlong theme. See below to understand how to use this book in different ways.

If your school wants to have one day a year called College Day.
• Read and follow the timeline on pages 9-10. There are forms, letters, and ideas that detail what can be done to implement a successful College Day in Chapter 1.

If your school wants to infuse a College Readiness theme at your school:
• Read and follow the timeline on pages 9-10. There are forms, letters, and ideas that detail what can be done to implement a successful College Day in Chapter 1.

• Read through Chapter 2 and choose some lessons that would work with your student population. Use PowerPoints from the CD (Overviews are included in Chapter 4) in some of these lessons.

• Display some bulletin boards around the school and encourage teachers to decorate their doors with ideas detailed in Chapter 3.

> **"EVERY STUDENT DESERVES THE OPPORTUNITY TO BE EDUCATED IN A WAY THAT PREPARES THEM FOR COLLEGE IF THEY SO CHOOSE TO ATTEND."**
> NO EXCUSES UNIVERSITY
> HTTP://NOEXCUSESU.COM

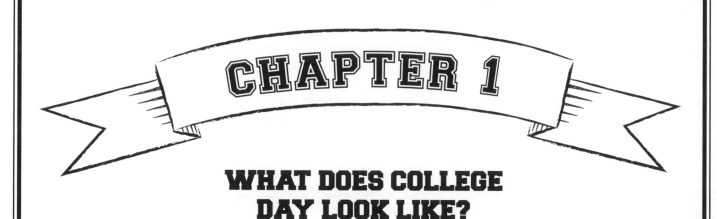

WHAT DOES COLLEGE DAY LOOK LIKE?

Many schools have a Career Day... but what about a College Day? Some educators might wonder how early is too early to start talking about college. An interesting statistic shows that if we talk to students about college for 5 minutes a day starting in Kindergarten, they will have thought about college 195 hours by the time they graduate high school. If we talk to a student about college for 5 minutes a day starting in 11th grade, they will have thought about college only 30 hours when they graduate high school (No Excuses University: http://noexcusesu. com). Why not present this information to young students so that they can set their sight high, gain knowledge, and enjoy a fun interactive day?

COLLEGE DAY LOOKS LIKE:

— Staff and students are encouraged to wear college attire.
— Classroom doors are decorated (see Chapter 3 for ideas)
— Classes are encouraged to do a college readiness activity or supplementary worksheet that day to generate discussion

The following list includes things that can be implemented on a College Day. One or two of these things can be added per year as the program grows.

• Round Robin of Speakers (see page 21)

• Family Members are invited to come to lunch wearing college gear (Lunchroom can be decorated accordingly)

• Announcements on school news can get the school excited and share College Readiness Facts (see page 32)

• Classes can be invited to a Tour of Doors and see all of the classroom door decorations

• Have a sign welcoming everyone to the school that day

• College Readiness lessons can be taught prior to the day

CHECKLIST TO CREATE A SUCCESSFUL COLLEGE DAY

At start of the year (or at least 2 months prior)

____ Get the buy-in from the leadership team and administration to go forward in creating a College Day.

____ Establish a date on the master calendar for your school for College Day (right before winter holidays or at the end of the year is a good time when teachers welcome a structured day and college students might be home to come help)

5-7 weeks prior

____ Send email or post in mailroom "Overview of College Day" to staff (page 11)

____ Recruit speakers for College Day Speakers (send out letter to potential speakers: template page 15, sample page 16)

____ Set deadline for door decorating contest and send out/put up in mailroom some examples (page 17 and examples in Chapter 3)

____ Implement college readiness lessons and do a student pre-post survey (pages 12-13)

3- 4 weeks prior

____ Send letter to parents/guardians inviting family members to come eat lunch with students on College Day (page 19)

____ Select College Helpers (or use a previously selected group i.e. Student Council, Peer Helpers, etc.)

1-2 weeks prior

____ Send reminder to College Day speakers (page 20)

____ Recruit door decoration judges (give them rubric on page 18)

____ Allow students (who are going to be participating in round robin of speakers) to choose courses (pages 21-23)

____ Train College Day Helpers (Agenda page 27 and signs for them to hold pages 28-29)

____ On school news/announcements record information about College Day

____ Make copies of worksheets that will be set out for teachers to peruse to supplement classroom activities (see Chapter 2)

____ Create a display of "We Went To College and So Can You" in a prominent place in the lobby/hallway (page 33)

____ Assign each speaker to a classroom and create a map of how the speaker rotation will proceed (see page 22 for template and page 23 for sample and page 25 for map)

The week of College Day

_____ Set out worksheets and supplementary printables in the mailroom so that teachers can make copies as desired (see Chapter 2)

_____ Ensure there is enough teacher/staff coverage in rooms with speakers

_____ Remind students that they can dress in college attire on College Day

The day before

_____ Resend maps of speakers

_____ Send registration of courses to staff (so that they know where students are located in the building and role can be called at courses)

_____ Buy bottled water for speakers

_____ Give door decoration judges deadline by which to judge doors (rubric on page 18)

_____ Remind teachers that on College Day they can take their class on a "Tour of Doors"

The day of

_____ Set up numbers outside the doors of speakers for easy visibility

_____ Set out folders and water for Speakers

_____ Carry walkie talkie so that you can communicate with office and other helpers

_____ Remind teachers to have students write Thank You Notes to speakers as a time for reflecting about what they learned (see page 63)

Follow up in the week following College Day

_____ Send out a Needs Assessment to teachers (see page 65)

COLLEGE DAY IS COMING!

WE ARE EXCITED FOR OUR UPCOMING COLLEGE DAY! PLEASE FEEL FREE TO SHARE ANY IDEAS AND FEEDBACK YOU MIGHT HAVE AS WE DEVELOP THE PROGRAM.

- ► All staff and students are invited to wear college apparel that day. In fact, tell your students now so that they know it is coming!

- ► A letter will go home telling students that they can invite relatives who are in college or vocational training to come have lunch with them and depending on how many reply, it's up to you if you want those people to come back to the room and talk to your students.

- ► There will be a door decorating contest.

- ► Wall displays will show where our staff went to college.

- ► Certain grade levels will have guest speakers. Details to come.

- ► We will have morning announcement/signs around school with trivia facts about post-secondary opportunities.

PRE/POST FOR STUDENTS

You can create something like this on surveymonkey.com, another online survey or even pen and paper. This survey is given to students prior to a lesson on college readiness and College Day, and then again afterwards. Also, this can be done in a lesson or if your teachers are on board, you can send them the web link and have kids rotate through the computer(s) in the room to complete the survey during morning work or an independent work time.

[PRE TEST]

1. How long does it usually take to graduate from a college or university?
- ◯ 1 year
- ◯ 2 years
- ◯ 4 years
- ◯ 6 years

2. What is a college course?
- ◯ A class
- ◯ An obstacle
- ◯ A race track
- ◯ A place to live

3. When someone gets a college degree, what does that mean?
- ◯ It means that they know how to tell the temperature.
- ◯ It means that they have taken enough classes to earn a certificate or diploma.
- ◯ It means that they will definitely get a job.
- ◯ It means that they like to learn.

4. A dormitory is _____.
- ◯ A building with rooms where students sleep.
- ◯ A place where you can do science experiments.
- ◯ A fitness center where students exercise.
- ◯ A cafeteria where meals can be eaten.

5. People who graduate from college typically make more money than those who do not graduate from college.
- ◯ True
- ◯ False

[POST TEST]

1. What was your favorite part about College Day?

_____

_____

2. What is a fact about college that you learned through College Day that you didn't know before?

_____

_____

3. Are you more likely to go to college now that you have learned more about it?
○ Yes
○ I'm just as likely to go to college as I was before
○ No

4. How long does it usually take to graduate from a college or university?
○ 1 year
○ 2 years
○ 4 years
○ 6 years

5. What is a college course?
○ A class
○ An obstacle
○ A race track
○ A place to live

6. When someone gets a college degree, what does that mean?
○ It means that they know how to tell the temperature.
○ It means that they have taken enough classes to earn a certificate or diploma.
○ It means that they will definitely will get a job.
○ It means that they like to learn.

7. A dormitory is _____.
○ A building with rooms where students sleep.
○ A place where you can do science experiments.
○ A fitness center where students exercise.
○ A cafeteria where meals can be eaten.

8. People who graduate from college typically make more money than those who do not graduate from college.
○ True
○ False

IDEAS OF SPEAKERS TO INVITE TO COLLEGE DAY

As you brainstorm ideas of who to invite for College Day, I encourage a careful selection of speakers that consists of a variety for kids to choose from. For example:

- Former alumni of your school

- Members of the armed forces

- Vocational school graduates

- High school counselors

- College admissions employees

- College/university professors

- People who received athletic scholarships

- First generation college students

- Adults who went back to college at a more mature age

- Chefs (who could have varied educational background)

- A college counselor

- A person who consults about where juniors should start looking at colleges

- A college student to talk about Greek life, dorm life, time management, making new friends, etc.

- Someone in graduate school

- A college employee who coordinates club sports

- Someone who is/was in college in the IT world

- Someone to discuss the impact of social media on college admissions

- An alumni representative of a popular school in your area

- A student teacher

- A student in an internship to discuss character traits that are important in school/work

- A bank representative to discuss the importance of budgeting and saving money

TEMPLATE OF LETTER FOR COLLEGE DAY SPEAKERS

Dear Potential College Day Volunteer,

This year at _____, we are having a College Day to help our students understand that post-secondary education is possible for all students. We want our students to have a sense of college readiness in understanding terms like "tuition, scholarship, dorms, semesters, vocational training, etc." We want them to hear from many different perspectives including current college students, people who have attended vocational school, those who are part of university staff, and college graduates.

We would love to invite you in to speak to our students about topics such as:

- How did you choose your college/school?
- Did you have a job before going to college/vocational school?
- Walk through a typical day in your life in college.
- Did you change what you wanted to study along the way?
- What was a fun part about being in school? What was difficult?
- What is the financial benefit to having post-secondary training?
- Feel free to bring in visuals of things you learned, assignments, photos, etc.

If possible, we are asking that you prepare a 20 minute presentation (which can really be 15 minutes with 5 minutes for questions at the end). We will have the students rotate speakers so that they can hear __ points of view.

To summarize, we want to invite you to come in on _____ from _____ until _____ . If possible please fill out the attached form or email me back your interest. We greatly appreciate you supporting the learning in our community.

Name of Staff
Name of School

- -

Please return this to (email) _____ by _____.

_____Yes I can join you on _____ from _____.

_____Unfortunately, I will not be able to make it to College Day.

Speaker's name _____

College/Vocational School _____

Your Contact Phone #_____   **email address** _____

Please let us know as soon as you can, if you are able to make it and you will then be contacted with further information!

SAMPLE OF LETTER TO COLLEGE DAY SPEAKER

Dear Potential College Day Volunteer,

This year at Blackwell Elementary, we are starting a College Day to bring in speakers to help our students understand that post-secondary education is possible for all students. We want our students to have a sense of college readiness in understanding terms like "tuition, scholarship, dorms, semesters, vocational training, etc." We want them to hear from many different perspectives.

We would love to invite you in to speak to our students about topics such as:

- How did you choose your college/school?
- Walk through a typical day in your life in college.
- Did you change what you wanted to study along the way?
- What was a fun part about being in school? What was difficult?
- What is the financial benefit to having post-secondary training?
- Feel free to bring in visuals of things you learned, assignments, photos, etc.

If possible, we are asking that you prepare a 20 minute presentation (which can really be 15 minutes with 5 minutes for questions at the end). We will have the students rotate speakers so that they can hear 2 points of view.

To summarize, we want to invite you to come in May 13th from 9:30-10:30 (1st Presentation will be 9:40-10:00 2nd Presentation of same material to different students 10:10-10:25). If possible please fill out the attached form or email me back your interest. We greatly appreciate you supporting the learning in our community.

Thanks for your consideration,
Lisa King, Ed.S
School Counselor, Blackwell Elementary School

- -

Please return this to lisa.king@cobbk12.org by Friday April 25, 2014.

_____Yes I can join you on May 13, 2014 from 9:30-10:30.

_____Unfortunately, I will not be able to make it on May 13, 2014.

Your name _____

College/Vocational School _____

Your Contact Phone #_____ **email address** _____

Please let us know as soon as you can, if you are able to make it and you will then be contacted with further information!

DOOR DECORATING CONTEST

One of the main functions of College Day and the college readiness curriculum is to create awareness that there are many post-secondary choices and college is one of those options. Having a door decorating contest is one way to make a school wide atmosphere in which education is important.

SAMPLE MEMO TO TEACHERS:

Teachers,

College Day is coming up in a few weeks. In order to promote our school wide belief in the importance in education, we will decorate our school with that message. The rubric that the judges will use includes the categories of:

Student-Involvement, Message, and Creativity.
Some ideas are posted in the _____ and you can use these ideas or create your own. Please complete your door by _____. Winners will be announced on _____ and classroom winners will receive a special prize.

COLLEGE DAY
DOOR DECORATING RUBRIC

	____CLASS	____CLASS	____CLASS	____CLASS	____CLASS	____CLASS
STUDENT-INVOLVEMENT						
CREATIVITY						
MESSAGE						
TOTAL						

COLLEGE DAY LUNCH INVITATION!

Dear Parents/Guardians,

We are excited to let you know about _____ School's College Day on _____. This day is about exposing our students to post-secondary educational opportunities. We know it is far in the future for our students, but we know that "Students with an eye on the future, do better in the present". On College Day, we are inviting students to wear apparel from any college, university, branch of the armed forces, vocational school, or training program that they would like.

We are encouraging students to invite family members or close family friends that are in college (or training programs) to come have lunch with them. Guests are also invited to wear the college shirts or hats.

This is our _____ annual College Day, and we are excited to invite our families and community members to help us reinforce to our students the importance of striving to dream big!

Thanks again for your support,

- -

Please fill this out to let us know if you or someone else will be joining your child for lunch on College Day on _____.

My child, _____, will be inviting

_____ to have lunch with him/her on College Day.

*Return this to your child's teacher to let them know you are coming.

"If we don't put the idea of college on the table early, the likelihood that kids are going to go to college is very low. It has to be part of their dream; you have to ingrain it in their plan for the future."

— Marta Tienda, Sociologist, Princeton University

_____ School

Dear College Day Volunteers,

Thank you very much for volunteering to speak at our College Round Robin on _____.
Please check into the office by _____ and a student will show you to the area where you
will be presenting. You will be speaking to _____ grade students. You will have two different
groups and approximately _____ minutes with each group. Each group will consist of approximately
20ish students. You will have a teacher and a student helper in your class at all times to help keep us all
on schedule. If you have any questions, please do not hesitate to call.

Here are some other ideas of things you can discuss in your presentation:
- How did you choose what college to attend?
- What was a typical day in your college like?
- Different jobs that your college education could have led to.
- Feel free to bring visuals, props, photos, books or assignments, websites etc.
- If you'd like, you can ask questions or play a game at the end of each session and give away any trinkets for answering questions about your presentation (a good way to see if they were listening!)
- Please let us know if you have any requests/needs.

If for some reason, a conflict arises and you cannot come, please call immediately so that we can plan
accordingly. We could not do this without the generosity of your time. On behalf of the students and
staff, thank you for your commitment to our community.

Sincerely,

Work _____   Cell _____

Email _____

Directions to School:

_____

_____

_____

HOW TO HELP STUDENTS CHOOSE COURSES

Prior to presenting courses to students, calculate how many students from each homeroom will sign up for each course. For example, if you have 10 speakers lined up and 9 classes from 4th and 5th grade participating in the speaker round robin, make sure that each speaker has students from each class. You may want to allow 2-4 kids from each room to sign up for each of the 10 speakers. Schedule a time for the students to make their selections.

Procedures for students choosing courses.

1. Counselor/Teacher can read this sample script to the students:
   "Students, you will be choosing a course just like a college student chooses his/her electives. "Electives" are courses that students can choose according to what they are interested in. Today, you will choose which speaker you would like to hear on College Day. You will be in a course with other students who are interested in this same topic. You might listen to a speaker who is a current college student or maybe someone who went to college years ago on a scholarship or maybe someone who takes online courses. Just as college students do, you will need to register for your course. When you are called on, you will tell me which course you would like to take or in other words, which speaker you would like to hear."

2. Counselor/Teacher will then show the students the menu of courses being offered (according to the speakers that have been invited).

3. Counselor/Teacher will tell students to choose a first choice and then a back-up choice.

4. Remind students that courses do fill up and a bell or sound will indicate when a course is full. Explain to the students that only 2-4 students from each class will be allowed in each course so that other classes have the opportunity to register for that speaker. This usually creates some grumbling, but the counselor/teacher can explain that this happens to everyone in college. A course fills up and you have to wait until the next semester to try and get into that course.

5. Counselor/Teacher can assign a supplemental activity (examples on pages 76-79) for the class to work on while each student is called on to register for a course. Courses will be crossed out as they are "filled" so that everyone knows what is left. Students who have good behavior can be chosen first (as a behavior modification tool).

FAQ

Q: Do students choose more than one course?

A: No. I have students rotate to the next speaker on the map (the room next door) to avoid chaotic scheduling. They have one chosen elective and then they will move to the room next door for the next session (and if there are 3 speakers, they keep rotating in order of the room numbers).

Q: How many students are in a group?

A: I try to keep the groups the size of an average class. This is why some of the speakers are "closed out" after a certain number of students sign up.

Q: Where are the teachers?

A: Classroom teachers are assigned to a group and travel with that group. If auxiliary staff is needed, they can be pulled in to supervise.

SAMPLE: COURSE OFFERINGS

For the students to select courses, I created an excel sheet like this (see template on page 23) with the speakers that I have recruited. I either embed it into a lesson or, as a separate 10 minute "drop in" to homerooms and allow the students to select courses (see page 21 for complete explanation).

COURSE OFFERINGS FOR COLLEGE DAY 2014

#	Course	Description
A	GOING BACK TO SCHOOL	Lucy is a mom of 3 kids, works part-time, and goes to college to get her degree. She will talk about why she decided to go back to school and how she balances all of her responsibilities. She is a great example of following your dreams.
B	BEING A COLLEGE PROFESSOR	Dr. A is a professor at GA State University in the Counseling Psychology department. He has his Ph.D. and teaches graduate students. Come hear what college courses are really like.
C	FIRST ONE TO GO TO COLLEGE	Hilda just finished her junior year at Mississippi State. She is the first one to go to college, has worked hard to be at school, and continues to succeed.
D	GOING TO LAW SCHOOL	Adam went to UGA and received his degree in journalism. He then decided to attend Law School and graduates from GA State this spring.
E	ATHLETIC SCHOLARSHIPS	Katie graduated from Furman University and was an athlete scholar on the basketball team. She will be speaking about being a student athlete and the success that comes from hard work.
F	EDUCATION OF A CHEF	Matt is the executive chef at a local restaurant and will be talking about the experience that helped him become a chef. He attended college in Chicago.
G	CLUB SPORTS IN COLLEGE	Sam attended this school when he was young. He graduated from KSU and now works there coordinating the club sports. He will talk about his college experience as well as the extra-curricular opportunities that college can provide.
H	GRADUATING FROM KSU	Hope is graduating from KSU with her teaching degree. She has been student teaching this year at Blackwell. She will talk about living in a dorm and other activities available for college students.
I	LIFE AT AUBURN UNIVERSITY	Rebecca just graduated from Auburn University. She was a student recruiter there and will tell you all about college life, living far from home, and the need to balance work and play.
J	HOW TO BUDGET YOUR MONEY	One of the difficult things about growing up is having to be responsible for yourself. Come learn about an important life skill that is essential in college and in life: learning to handle money.

SAMPLE: Course Offerings

COURSE OFFERINGS FOR COLLEGE DAY		
COURSE A	**COURSE F**	
COURSE B	**COURSE G**	
COURSE C	**COURSE H**	
COURSE D	**COURSE I**	
COURSE E	**COURSE J**	

Education is the most powerful weapon which you can use to change the world. — Nelson Mandela

STUDENT SIGN UP FOR COURSES

STUDENTS SIGNED UP FOR THIS COURSE																LOCATION OF COURSE/STAFF SUPERVISING	
																	COURSE A
																	COURSE B
																	COURSE C
																	COURSE D
																	COURSE E
																	COURSE F
																	COURSE G

SAMPLE OF MAP/SCHEDULE FOR SPEAKERS

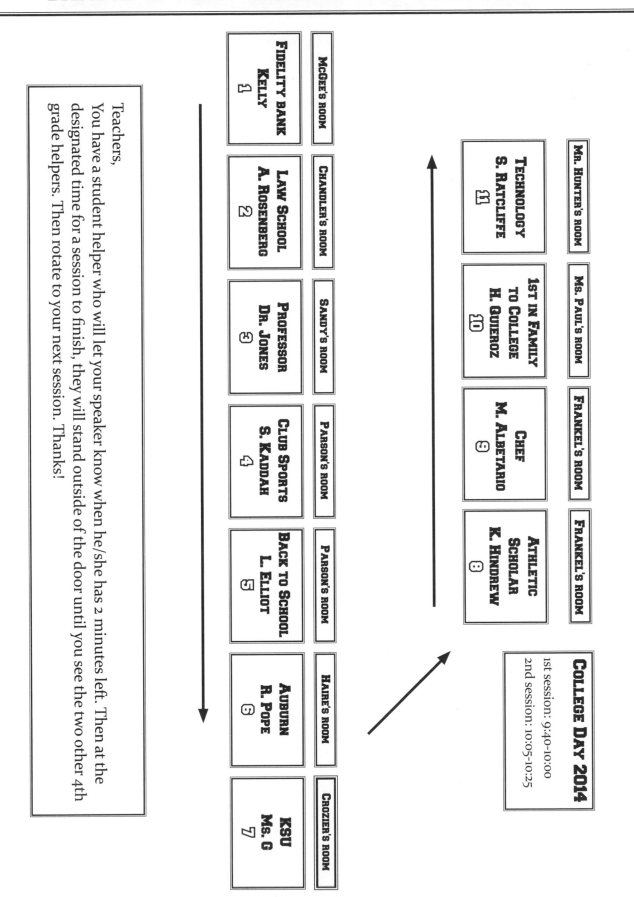

McGee's Room

FIDELITY BANK
KELLY
1

Chandler's Room

LAW SCHOOL
A. ROSENBERG
2

Sandy's Room

PROFESSOR
DR. JONES
3

Parson's Room

CLUB SPORTS
S. KADDAH
4

Parson's Room

BACK TO SCHOOL
L. ELLIOT
5

Haire's Room

AUBURN
R. POPE
6

Crozier's Room

KSU
MS. G
7

Mr. Hunter's Room

TECHNOLOGY
S. RATCLIFFE
11

Ms. Paul's Room

1ST IN FAMILY
TO COLLEGE
H. QUIEROZ
10

Frankel's Room

CHEF
M. ALBETARIO
9

Frankel's Room

ATHLETIC
SCHOLAR
K. HINDREW
8

COLLEGE DAY 2014

1st session: 9:40–10:00
2nd session: 10:05–10:25

Teachers,
You have a student helper who will let your speaker know when he/she has 2 minutes left. Then at the designated time for a session to finish, they will stand outside of the door until you see the two other 4th grade helpers. Then rotate to your next session. Thanks!

OVERVIEW OF COLLEGE DAY HELPERS:

College Day is an exciting day. There are many students who would be great helpers and assist in making career day more organized.

— Who do you choose as a helper and how many helpers should you have?

It is important for college helpers to be responsible and have the ability to tell time to help keep the speakers on schedule. The size of your school and how many classes you have in each grade level will determine how many helpers you have. Typically having one college helper per volunteer speaker is effective.

— How do you choose College Day helpers?

As the organizer, you can either hand pick helpers or you could have students submit a paragraph on "Why is learning about college important?" and select helpers from this activity. Also, you can simply have the teachers select one or two responsible students in their class to be a college helper.

Sample Letter for College Day Helpers

Dear Parent/Guardian:

Congratulations! Your child has been selected as a College Day Helper. College Day Helpers are responsible students who will help the counselors greet speakers and help to keep our speakers on schedule. We will have a training session so that your child knows just what to do on College Day, which is on _____. College Day Helpers will participate in the day just like the rest of the students, but they will serve as leaders. We appreciate their help and congratulate them on being selected!

Sincerely,

COLLEGE DAY HELPERS AGENDA

Welcome and Congratulations on being selected as a College Day helper.

- **How to greet your College Day Speaker**

  — "Hello, and welcome to our school. Thank you for coming to College Day. My name is _____. Do you have any questions about the day?"

  — Give them the provided bottle of water, a copy of their schedule and walk them to their classroom.

- **What are my responsibilities on that day?**

  — You will come to the lobby to greet your speaker and walk them to their room.

  — In the classrooms, you will serve as a "timer" for the speaker. When there are two minutes left in the session, you will have a sign that you will hold up to remind the speaker of the time limit.

- **When are you to come to the lobby to greet your speaker?**

  — Meet me in the lobby at _____

COLLEGE DAY HELPERS ARE RESPONSIBLE STUDENTS WHO WILL HELP THE COUNSELORS GREET SPEAKERS AND HELP TO KEEP OUR SPEAKERS ON SCHEDULE.

YOU HAVE 2 MORE MINUTES IN YOUR PRESENTATION.

EXCUSE ME, BUT OUR TIME IS UP! THANKS!

WELCOME

THANKS FOR COMING TO COLLEGE DAY.
I WILL SHOW YOU WHERE YOU WILL BE DOING
YOUR PRESENTATION.

THANKS AGAIN!

COLLEGE DAY HELPER REMINDER NOTE

Send these to the helpers that have been selected. Choose at least one helper per speaker:

Thank you for helping out as a College Day Helper!
Please meet me in the lobby at _____ tomorrow,
_____. Thanks!

Thank you for helping out as a College Day Helper!
Please meet me in the lobby at _____ tomorrow,
_____. Thanks!

Thank you for helping out as a College Day Helper!
Please meet me in the lobby at _____ tomorrow,
_____. Thanks!

COLLEGE DAY HELPERS WILL PARTICIPATE IN THE DAY JUST LIKE THE REST OF THE STUDENTS, BUT THEY WILL SERVE AS LEADERS

ANNOUNCEMENTS FOR THE SCHOOL NEWS, ETC.

If your school has closed circuit video or an intercom, use this forum to promote career and college readiness. Here are some ideas for the morning announcements:

• Highlight a university each day.

• Have staff make appearances to discuss where they went to college.

• Play a fight song from a particular school and play "name that university."

• Have students with siblings in college interview them and read the interview.

• Have a graffiti board where students can write about where they hope to attend.

• Announce college trivia questions and award prizes to winners.

• Select a student to be on a College Crew throughout the year to do features such as reporting college facts or interviewing different people about their college on the school news.

• Announce that College attire/shirts can be worn on one Friday a month.

• Interview kids around the school about what they think words mean and then tell the real meaning.

SAMPLE: ANNOUNCEMENTS THE WEEK OF COLLEGE DAY!

MONDAY: We are so excited for College Day this week which is on _____. Don't forget that you can wear your college shirts or hats on that day. Listen each morning this week for interesting facts.

TUESDAY: You might think that you are too young to think about college, but you are not! It is never too early to concentrate on working hard and setting goals for your future. Many people think that kids with their eye on the future do better in the present. We think they are right!

WEDNESDAY: There are many different choices you will have after high school. There are 2 year colleges, the armed forces, 4 year colleges/universities, or vocational schools. As you get older you will explore what decision is right for you. For now it is important to know, that if you work hard, you can achieve your goals.

THURSDAY: In college, you choose a major. This means that you choose what you want to study. If you major is Technology, you concentrate your learning on computers. If you go to college what do you think you would want to major in?

FRIDAY: If you decide to go to college, there are so many choices. You could take classes online or in a classroom, you could go to a large university with 25,000 students or a smaller college. You can go to a school with a big football team, or no team at all. You get to make the choices about what goals you have for yourself. If you work hard enough, you might even get money to help you go to college (called a scholarship). The sky is the limit and we hope that you have enjoyed this week of exploring the possibilities.

WE WENT TO COLLEGE AND SO CAN YOU!

MATERIALS: outlines of states (found on CD), map of the USA (can be printed out from internet graphic or purchased)

PROCEDURES:

1. Send out email to staff asking where they went to college.

2. Type or write staff members names within the shape/outline of the state in which they went to school.

WHERE DID OUR STAFF GRADUATE FROM COLLEGE?

HOW MANY STAFF MEMBERS ATTENDED COLLEGE IN EACH OF THESE STATES?

List 9 different states across the bottom.

	more than 20	20	19	18	17	16	15	14	13	12	11	10	9	8	7	6	5	4	3	2	1

WHERE DID OUR STAFF GRADUATE FROM COLLEGE?

NAME _____

TEACHER NAME _____

1. How many staff members graduated from a college in the state in which you live?

_____

_____

_____

2. What are the states in which only one staff member graduated college?

_____

_____

_____

3. Which staff member(s) went to college the furthest away from the state in which you live?

_____

_____

_____

4. Which state has the most graduates listed?

_____

_____

_____

[REPRODUCIBLE]

COLLEGE DAY SCAVENGER HUNT

NAME _____

DIRECTIONS: This scavenger hunt will require you to talk to some staff members, fellow students, and to look around the school building.

GET THE SIGNATURE OF A STUDENT WHO WANTS TO GO TO MEDICAL SCHOOL AND BECOME A DOCTOR.	**WHAT STAFF MEMBER IS TAKING A COLLEGE COURSE RIGHT NOW?**
WHERE IN THE BUILDING IS A PICTURE OF A COLLEGE MASCOT LOCATED?	**WHAT TYPE OF DEGREE DOES YOUR PRINCIPAL HAVE?**
WHERE IN THE BUILDING IS A MASTER'S DEGREE DIPLOMA HUNG ON A WALL?	**WHERE DID YOUR TEACHER GO TO COLLEGE?**
WHERE IS THE WORD "COLLEGE" LOCATED IN THE BUILDING?	**GET THE SIGNATURE OF A PERSON WHO LIVED IN A DORM IN COLLEGE.**
WHERE IN THE BUILDING IS A BACHELOR'S DEGREE HUNG ON A WALL?	**ASK A STAFF MEMBER HOW MANY PEOPLE IN THIS BUILDING HAVE EARNED A DOCTORAL DEGREE PhD.**
GET THE SIGNATURE OF A STUDENT WHO HAS A FAVORITE COLLEGE FOOTBALL TEAM.	**GET THE SIGNATURE OF A STUDENT WHO WANTS TO GO TO CULINARY SCHOOL AND BECOME A CHEF.**
WRITE DOWN THE YEAR THAT YOU WILL GRADUATE HIGH SCHOOL.	**GET THE SIGNATURE OF A PERSON WHO HAD A JOB WHILE THEY WERE ATTENDING COLLEGE.**

©YouthLight [37]

COLLEGE DAY

Please take a copy of any of these supplemental activities to reinforce our upcoming:

Please take a copy of any of these supplemental activities to reinforce our upcoming:

COLLEGE DAY

SIGN TO PUT NEAR WORKSHEETS

STUDENT TEMPLATE FOR THANK YOU NOTES TO SPEAKERS

THANK YOU

DEAR _____ ,

_____

_____

_____

_____

_____

_____

_____

_____

_____

_____

_____

ON YOUR LETTERHEAD

Thank you so much for coming to _____'s College Day. We could not have had such a successful day without you sharing your time with us. The children learned so much about different post-secondary experiences and had a great time in the process. Students and teachers gave wonderful feedback about this fantastic day of learning. Enclosed are some cards the students made to show their appreciation for your time and support.

Thanks again for your contribution,

NEEDS ASSESSMENT

After College Day, it is important to assess what went well and what needs tweaking for the next year. This survey can be done online with surveymonkey.com or Google docs, or in paper pencil form.

GRADE LEVEL _____

1. I think College Day (during the last week or so of school) is a good addition to our school as a tradition and learning experience.

☐ Yes

☐ No

2. Please rate the following activities:

	DEFINITELY CONTINUE	POTENTIALLY CONTINUE	UNSURE IF IT WAS EFFECTIVE
Door Decoration Contest			
Speakers (for those teachers who participated)			
Inviting Family to Lunch			
Stickers for Kids			
Map Display of Where Teachers went to College			

3. Other suggestions/comments/feedback regarding College Day:

_____

_____

_____

_____

DATA REPORT

This is an example of a data report that can be developed to share the positive results of a program that incorporates College Readiness.

LESSON TOPIC: COLLEGE READINESS SKILLS	SCHOOL YEAR: 2013-14

PURPOSE: To expose students to the notion of post-secondary education and empower them with the notion that college is a possibility for the future.

GOAL: The goal of the counseling curriculum is to expose students to the different post-secondary options of further education. After participating in the lesson and College Day experience, students will have increased knowledge of college vocabulary by 15 % and have increased their perception of viewing college as a feasible option by 25%.

INTENDED STUDENT OUTCOME: The intended outcome is to increase student perception of viewing college as a feasible option by 25%.

GRADE LEVELS: 4TH START AND END DATES: APRIL-MAY 2014	PROCESS DATA # OF STUDENTS AFFECTED: 125

PROCEDURES

LESSON CONTENT AND ACTIVITIES (WHAT WERE THE SPECIFICS OF THE LESSONS DELIVERED?):
A PowerPoint presentation/lesson was delivered to each 4th grade class. Students guessed what the word was for certain definitions (i.e.: What is a college class called? course; What is the housing called where students live on campus? dormitory)

LESSON PRESENTED IN WHICH CLASS/SUBJECT: Lessons were presented for 30 minutes in each 4th grade class. Two weeks after the lesson, students participated in College Day where they attended two sessions (20 minutes each) where they heard different aspects of post-secondary education.

HOW WAS IT ASSESSED (HOW DID YOU DETERMINE IF THE DELIVERY OF THE CURRICULUM WAS SUCCESSFUL?): Teachers and students completed a survey on surveymonkey.com to assess the effectiveness of the lessons and the College Day program. (Staff Responses n= 34)
Student Responses Pre N= 47 Post N=39)

RESULTS

Perception data (changes in attitude, skills, and/or knowledge):

STUDENT VOCABULARY WORD KNOWLEDGE	PRE	POST	CHANGE
Students knew what the word "dormitory" meant	78	94	21%
Students knew what the word "course" meant	83	87	5%

ARE YOU MORE LIKELY TO GO TO COLLEGE NOW THAT YOU HAVE LEARNED MORE ABOUT IT?

Student Responses	Yes	I'm just as likely to go to college as I was before	No
	66.77%	30.77%	2.56%

DATA REPORT

STAFF NEEDS ASSESSMENT ABOUT COLLEGE DAY:	DEFINITELY CONTINUE	POTENTIALLY CONTINUE	NOT SURE IF THIS WAS EFFECTIVE
Door Decoration	76.47%	23.53%	0.00%
Speakers (for those teachers who participated)	95.83%	0.00%	4.17%
Inviting Family to Lunch	60.61%	18.18%	21.21%
Stickers for Kids	69.70%	12.12%	18.18%
Map Display of Where Teachers went to School	88.24%	8.82%	2.94%
I think College Day is a good addition to our school as a tradition and learning experience.	97%	3%	0%

Number of Community Members who came to our building to help us learn and celebrate College Day:
- 11 Speakers
- 26 Guests who came to eat with students wearing college attire (approximate #)

SUMMARY AND CONCLUSIONS

What have you concluded from the delivery of the curriculum? The premise of presenting College Readiness Curriculum to younger students aligns with the quote "Kids with their eye on the future do better in the present." According to data and feedback, this was a very successful program that will be continued next year. Some of the open ended questions in survey monkey indicated that staff and students would want to see 3 speakers instead of 2 speakers in their round robin rotation. The most encouraging data point came from the student response that 67% of them believe that after hearing more about college, they are more likely to go to college.

FUTURE PLANS

Based on your conclusions, what is your next step? Based on the positive responses from staff, students, and parents College Day will be an annual program that we offer at Blackwell, and we will expand the program with ideas that were inspired from this year.

Ideas of Prizes to Give for Contest/Incentives

Below are ideas for prizes that can be given for contests, for good behavior during lessons, for each kid to have (depending on size of classes).

Note that if these particular things are not available, just do an internet search for the description and you may find something similar or new to give away!

Plush Bears with cap and gown:

http://www.orientaltrading.com/plush-graduation-bears-a2-38_42.fltr?prodCatId=550202+1256

Diploma Roll Candy

http://www.orientaltrading.com/diploma-roll-candy-a2-38_563.fltr?prodCatId=551290+1256

Graduation Cap Eraser Pencil Toppers

http://www.centurynovelty.com/detail_146-1972__89.html

Graduation Bubbles

http://www.centurynovelty.com/items_233__Favors-Toys-Gifts.html

Graduations Bubbles Necklace

http://www.partycity.com/product/graduation+party+favors.do

OTHER IDEAS FOR COLLEGE DAY, COLLEGE WEEK AND COLLEGE AWARENESS

- Assign students a post-secondary institution to research and report about the sports, activities, tuition, etc.

- Have staff members bring in photos of themselves in college.

- Have student write letters or e-mail professors of local colleges to send your students information, visit your classroom to assist with a lesson or give a talk.

- Obtain maps from different colleges/universities and encourage teachers to incorporate these in map skills lessons.

- Staff members can wear college/university t-shirts/hats.

- Have a "Wall of Fame" in the school hallway where photos of famous individuals are posted along with the name of the college or university that they attended.

- Have an egg hunt with the names of schools inside the eggs. Students that get the greatest number of schools collected win a prize. (Students can label these schools on a map to integrate some map skills.)

- Have students sign promissory notes or pledges to attend college or post-secondary training.

- Coordinate a trip to a local college campus. If unable to go there, maybe do a virtual tour with google maps.

- Teachers in each classroom name their table groups/areas after a certain college or university.

- Decorate the cafeteria with table tents and decorations of different colleges.

- Have your students call you "Professor _____" for the day instead of "Mrs./Mr. _____".

- Watch video clips (see page 46) and have students do a written response. One example is a true story describing a boy in Africa who was forced to drop out of school. It is about the power of being a self-motivated learner. Also, this would be a good prompt about, "What education means to me."

- Have books available in the media center for check out (see pages 48-49). One example is *Ruby's Wish* that takes place in China, at a time when few girls are taught to read or write, Ruby dreams of going to the university with her brothers and male cousins.

- Have students write letters to admissions offices at a college telling them why they should be admitted to that college(see page 78).

- Go on a "Tour of Doors" to see all of the fabulous creativity that inspires further education.

- Create "Mock College Electives" for older students. Anyone on staff such as support staff, nurses, teachers, administrators and counselors can design high interest courses that result in a tangible product. (Example topics are "History of Legos", "Ancestry" and "Advertising".) This can give students a true feel of what it is like to take an elective in college. Two weeks before the event, students select the classes that interest them most from a list of course descriptions. From their first, second, and third choices, class lists and student schedules for College Day can be created.

OTHER IDEAS FOR COLLEGE DAY, COLLEGE WEEK AND COLLEGE AWARENESS (CONT.)

- Each class "adopts" a college for the year. Decorate your classrooms with college themed props.

- Create a mini museum where staff members create a college display from their respective universities.

- Do random drawing giveaways of college paraphernalia (pencils, pens, cups etc.) Have staff write their alma maters to acquire pennants and other materials that could be used for this initiative, or staff can use this as an opportunity for students to write their colleges.

- Have a family night around the theme of Monsters University. Incorporate a lot of college info and activities. Create a scavenger hunt where families move through activity stations to find out facts about college.

- Invite a mascot from a local college to visit your school.

WEBSITES AND VIDEO LINKS

MONSTERS UNIVERSITY HAS ITS OWN WEBSITE THAT IS INTERACTIVE, ENTERTAINING, AND INFORMATIVE:

http://monstersuniversity.com/edu/

VIDEO LINKS OF STORIES OF STUDENTS SUCCEEDING POST COLLEGE AND BEATING THE ODDS.

http://youcango.collegeboard.org/stories

ARTICLE PUBLISHED ONLINE: DECEMBER 7, 2010 ELEMENTARY STUDENTS ENCOURAGED TO SET COLLEGE GOALS:

http://www.edweek.org/ew/articles/2010/12/08/14colleges_ep.h30.html?tkn=LYQFB H8ogSTsm%2FNzDR4uqSYEF53ArnVogJT5&intc=es

A SEARCH-FINDER TO LOOK FOR COLLEGES AT COLLEGE 411:

http://www.collegedata.com/cs/search/college/college_search_tmpl.jhtml

MICHELLE OBAMA TALKING ABOUT BEING THE FIRST ONE TO GO TO COLLEGE IN HER FAMILY.

https://www.youtube.com/watch?v=RYsQp_ocMvQ (1:49 minutes)

PEOPLE LIKE ME

https://www.youtube.com/watch?v=4pnW7Oel7ak (2:19)

WILL SMITH MOTIVATIONAL SPEECH

https://www.youtube.com/watch?v=Ucv8O75erpg

A GREAT SHORT VIDEO SHOWING STUDENTS TO "TAKE ACTION". YOU KNOW WHAT TO DO... SO DO IT!

https://www.youtube.com/watch?v=VrSUe_m19FY

A VIDEO EXPLAINING WHAT TUITION IS:

http://video.about.com/collegesavings/Quick-Tip--What-is-Tuition-.htm

ARTICLE ABOUT HOW JOBS AND HOBBIES ARE IMPORTANT IN COLLEGE APPLICATIONS:

http://www.usnews.com/education/best-colleges/articles/2013/11/12/incorporate-jobs-hobbies-into-college-applications?src=usn_fb

A GREAT WEBSITE ON THE IMPORTANCE OF EARLY EXPOSURE TO COLLEGE READINESS:

http://nosca.collegeboard.org/eight-components/college-aspirations

CHAPTER 2

LESSONS TO ENHANCE COLLEGE READINESS SKILLS

Although thoughts of post-secondary education are far away, elementary students get excited when they learn about college and other post-secondary opportunities. These lessons will be helpful to teach basic college readiness skills, goal setting, or to inspire students to think about their future.

The object of education is to prepare the young to educate themselves for their life.
– Robert M. Hutchins

BIBILOTHERAPY:
BOOKS THAT REINFORCE THE IMPORTANCE OF EDUCATION

Below are books that will correlate with lessons about the importance of education. There is a line before each book so that you can mark where it is located, so that if you decide to use it in a lesson you know where to find it. (Personal Library, Media Center, audiobook online, Public Library, or Need to Order it)

_____*Mahalia Mouse Goes to College: Book and CD by John Lithgow* —Mahalia Mouse lives underneath an old Harvard dormitory. Looking for food, Mahalia gets stuck in a backpack and finds herself in a classroom far from home. She is fascinated by the class and soon becomes a full-time student. As Mahalia learns, your students will gain insight into the world of college.

BOOKS ABOUT THE LOVE OF KNOWLEDGE

_____*Seeds of Change* by Jen Cullerton Johnson – This is a great book to show children that there are parts of the world where girls are not able to receive a formal education.

_____*Ruby's Wish* by Shirin Yim – Ruby is unlike most girls in China. Instead of aspiring to get married, Ruby wants to attend university just like the boys in her family. Based on the story of the author's grandmother, this is a story of a young girl who strives for an education.

_____*Miss Dorothy and Her Bookmobile* by Gloria Houston – When Dorothy was young, she loved books and wanted to be a librarian but there is no library in her town. Dorothy and her neighbors decide to start a bookmobile so that she could bring the books to people at school, on the farm, even in the middle of a river. This is a story about perseverance and how books and knowledge can change people's lives.

_____*Beatrice's Goat* by Lori Lohstoeter – Beatrice wants to be a schoolgirl more than any thing, but in her village, only children who can afford uniforms and books can go to school. Her family is much too poor. When Beatrice receives a goat as a gift from some people far away her future just might take a different path.

_____*Incredible Book Eating Boy* by Oliver Jeffers – One day Henry gets a craving to eat a book. Pretty soon he is eating volumes, and the information goes straight to his brain. He has hopes of becoming the smartest person in the world. When his taste for books disappears, he figures out another way to get smart that isn't so rough on the stomach. This book introduces the concept that nothing can take the place of hard work.

_____*The Boy Who Harnessed the Wind* by William Kamkwamba – A true story of a boy who at 14 years old built a windmill in his village using pictures from a book in the library. This is a great book to reinforce the notion that a great idea and a lot of hard work can change lives (see page 64).

_____*Hello Hello* by Mathew Cordell – This picture book delivers a message to step away from technology long enough to connect with nature and one another. This is a great hook for a lesson on the impact of technology. (Discussions could be re: Social Media impact on college admissions or the importance of being technology savvy but also a well-rounded student)

_____ ***Roberto, The Insect Architect* by Nina Laden** – Roberto does not quite fit in with his termite friends. He dreams of building with wood instead of eating it. Roberto leaves for the city in search of his dream to become an architect. His first project has him working at a drafting table, busily drawing blueprints for a milk-carton shelter and finally achieving his dreams.

Books Celebrating Looking Forward and Dreaming Big

_____ ***The World Belongs to You* by Ricardo Bozzi** – A book with simple text in which students will grasp the bigger meaning. This book is great for end of the year, transition to middle school, or thinking about future goals.

_____ ***I Knew You Could: A Book For All The Stops In Your Life* by Craig Dorfman** – This book is a great way to impart the message to students, "I know that you will be successful as you move on in life." This book features a little engine that we always knew could… and is a great metaphor for seeking higher learning.

_____ ***Yay You! Moving Up and Moving On* by Sandra Boynton** – This book is short and sweet and covers just about everything about moving forward in life, from careers to friends. "There are so many choices./The world is immense./Take a good look around/and decide what makes sense."

_____ ***Oh the Places You'll Go!* By Dr. Seuss** – The whimsical voice of Dr. Seuss gives a great outline for a discussion about moving ahead in life regardless of what stage of life.

_____ ***Curious George You're On your Way* by H.A. Rey** – This book is a perfect send off for people of all ages entering a new phase of life. Curious George goes through many of his classic scenes and gives great advice for the road in life ahead.

_____ ***Reach for the Stars* by Serge Bloch** – This is a great book to celebrate accomplishments with words of advice for those moving on to a different stage in life.

_____ ***If You Hold a Seed* by Ellie MacKay** – This book is about a boy who discovers the magic of what happens when a seed is planted in the ground. It takes sun, rain and patience, but eventually the boy notices leaves on the tree. The boy and tree get bigger and the book goes on to give great metaphors for the growth of trees to be used. (Watch me grow project)

_____ ***Big Plans* by Bob Shea** – This story is about a little boy who ponders the possibilities of the future. He has big plans. This would be a good lead in to a lesson asking students what their big plans are for the future.

_____ ***Line 135* by Germano Zullo** – Combines a whimsical story with and philosophical message.

COUNSELOR CONNECTION CARD

DIRECTIONS: After a lesson on College Awareness is taught, give each student a copy of the counselor connection card below. If they bring it back by a designated date, they are eligible to win a prize. You can draw three of the counselor connection cards that have been returned and those students are given a prize. (See College Related Prizes ideas on page 43.)

 COUNSELOR CONNECTION CARD:
College/Vocational Training Awareness

This week in our counselor curriculum lesson, we reviewed the concept of why education is important. Talk to your child about what training you have had. What type of training have you had that has helped you at a job? What classes have you taken to broaden your skills?

Signing this Counselor Connection Card means you have discussed with your child why education and training are important.

Student Name _____

Homeroom _____

Adult Signature _____

 COUNSELOR CONNECTION CARD:
College/Vocational Training Awareness

This week in our counselor curriculum lesson, we reviewed the concept of why education is important. Talk to your child about what training you have had. What type of training have you had that has helped you at a job? What classes have you taken to broaden your skills?

Signing this Counselor Connection Card means you have discussed with your child why education and training are important.

Student Name _____

Homeroom _____

Adult Signature _____

 COUNSELOR CONNECTION CARD:
College/Vocational Training Awareness

This week in our counselor curriculum lesson, we reviewed the concept of why education is important. Talk to your child about what training you have had. What type of training have you had that has helped you at a job? What classes have you taken to broaden your skills?

Signing this Counselor Connection Card means you have discussed with your child why education and training are important.

Student Name _____

Homeroom _____

Adult Signature _____

 COUNSELOR CONNECTION CARD:
College/Vocational Training Awareness

This week in our counselor curriculum lesson, we reviewed the concept of why education is important. Talk to your child about what training you have had. What type of training have you had that has helped you at a job? What classes have you taken to broaden your skills?

Signing this Counselor Connection Card means you have discussed with your child why education and training are important.

Student Name _____

Homeroom _____

Adult Signature _____

[REPRODUCIBLE]

COLLEGE READINESS CROSSWORD PUZZLE

ACROSS

2. A student chooses a _____ which will be the focus of a student's studies.
3. The land on which a college is located.
7. Where a student might live on campus.
8. A _____ often goes to culinary school to learn cooking skills.
9. Some people choose to work before going to college to get on-the-job _____.

DOWN

1. Another name for a college class
4. Many brave young men and women enlist in the _____ forces after finishing high school.
5. The first year of college is called your _____ year.
6. If you have a college degree, you are likely to make more _____

CRYPTOGRAM

NAME _____

DIRECTIONS: This puzzle is called a Cryptogram. At the top there is a KEY that lists all the letters used in the puzzle with a box below. Each of the letters has a corresponding number; some are already shown. Fill in the letters that correspond to the numbers below the blanks to solve the phrase.

KEY:

A	B	C	D	E	F	G	H	I	J	K	L	M	N	O	P	Q	R	S	T	U	V	W	X	Y	Z
1							15								24	25	20							5	

T H __   __ __ __ T   __ A Y   T __
20 15 7   14 7 22 20   19 1 5   20 11

P R __ __ __ __ T
24 25 7 18 17 21 20

T H __   __ __ T __ R __   __ __   T __
20 15 7   4 12 20 12 25 7   17 22   20 11

__ R __ A T __   __ T.
21 25 7 1 20 7   17 20

[REPRODUCIBLE]

PUZZLE:
COLLEGE READINESS WORD SEARCH

NAME _____

```
B  N  O  I  T  I  U  T  I  A  C  H  M  J  R
D  B  W  Y  O  Z  S  R  Y  O  G  Y  G  Q  E
A  O  G  Q  P  A  V  N  L  Q  M  I  V  O  A
S  G  R  S  C  H  O  L  A  R  S  H  I  P  D
K  U  R  M  Z  J  E  I  E  T  J  T  R  U  I
U  E  P  V  I  G  G  E  U  O  F  N  B  J  N
B  T  G  M  E  T  R  I  U  C  U  L  Y  N  E
Z  X  K  O  A  G  O  Z  C  S  Q  X  E  B  S
J  D  L  N  E  C  M  R  K  A  B  Z  R  N  S
W  A  C  D  T  X  B  Q  Y  M  H  X  F  C  P
I  I  V  I  P  O  P  C  L  V  O  C  U  V  S
H  N  D  L  K  U  Q  E  S  M  B  U  Q  U  Y
P  V  K  V  F  L  C  O  U  R  S  E  K  N  E
P  A  W  E  E  B  M  E  W  D  B  G  J  Q  S
F  Z  H  M  W  I  W  L  D  H  C  S  T  K  X
```

CAMPUS	COLLEGE	COURSE
DEGREE	DORMITORY	MASCOT
READINESS	SCHOLARSHIP	TUITION

[REPRODUCIBLE]

WHAT COMES AFTER HIGH SCHOOL WORD SEARCH

NAME _____

DIRECTIONS: The words below all have to do with training or education you might need when you get older. See how many words you can find.

```
T  T  P  Y  N  S  B  B  B  L  T  D  Q  Y  Q
Z  R  I  Y  R  O  T  I  M  R  O  D  G  R  R
I  A  H  K  T  I  I  G  H  C  O  O  O  E  L
N  I  S  R  A  I  U  T  T  U  L  J  T  X  C
T  N  R  O  H  L  N  O  A  O  W  S  A  O  R
E  I  A  W  E  E  R  U  N  C  E  N  L  M  E
R  N  L  S  J  A  X  H  M  M  I  L  X  F  T
N  G  O  E  T  I  C  P  E  M  E  L  I  C  A
S  C  H  E  N  E  W  S  E  G  O  L  P  V  U
H  E  C  Z  T  U  K  J  E  R  P  C  J  P  D
I  P  S  U  N  I  V  E  R  S  I  T  Y  T  A
P  V  O  C  A  T  I  O  N  C  E  E  O  O  R
O  S  R  E  T  S  A  M  K  L  T  Y  N  R  G
J  U  N  W  H  X  R  L  X  G  E  D  E  C  T
T  R  H  O  Y  F  I  U  R  B  T  R  Q  N  E
```

APPLICATION	COLLEGE	COMMUNITY	WORK
DOCTORATE	DORMITORY	EXPERIENCE	VOCATION
GED	GRADUATE	INTERNSHIP	UNIVERSITY
LIFE	MAJOR	MASTERS	SCHOLARSHIP
SEMESTER	TECHNOLOGY	TRAINING	

WHAT TRAINING WILL I NEED?
LESSONS AND WORKSHEETS

OVERVIEW: This lesson will teach students about different types of post-secondary training and make students more aware about different avenues that are possible.

MATERIALS: Worksheet on page 57 to make flip flap book, colored pencils/markers, writing utensils, scissors, envelopes with titles. Alternative to Worksheets

PROCEDURES:

1. Ask student to get into groups of 2-4 students.

2. Distribute to each group a ziploc bag filled with: letter sized envelopes labeled "College," "On the Job Training," "Vocational/Technical School," "Advanced Graduate Degree" and "I don't know," and strips of paper with names of careers (see worksheet on page 56).

3. Have the children sort the strips of paper into the envelopes. Discuss that some jobs require a specific degree while some careers can be done without any specific level of training.

4. After the groups are finished with the activity, review the correct answers to the sort activity, and write them on the board. (Note that some jobs can require different levels of training. For instance a chef can have on-the-job training or vocation school and a teacher has to have at least college education, but a lawyer has to have graduate school). When reviewing answers give the explanation that there might be more than one correct answer.

5. Next, students will create a flip flap book (page 57 for template) about different types of training. Students can choose 3 of the types of training and then draw a picture of a career that belongs in each category.

Extension: Have a list of career clusters. Assign each team a career cluster and have each team make a flip flap book for that cluster. For example in the health sciences, on-the-job training is a med tech, college is a nurse, advanced-degree is a nurse or doctor.

WHAT TRAINING WILL I NEED WORKSHEET

Students: Cut out the jobs below and sort them into categories: "College," "On-the Job Training," "Vocational/Technical School," "Advanced Graduate Degree" and "I don't know."

LAWYER	SALESMAN	ADMINISTRATIVE ASSISTANT
DENTAL HYGIENIST	MECHANIC	PLUMBER
VETERINARIAN	FARMER	VIDEO GAME DESIGNER
SCHOOL COUNSELOR	WELDER	ACTOR
NURSE	PROFESSIONAL ATHLETE	CHEF
HAIR STYLIST	AUTHOR	CASHIER

[REPRODUCIBLE]

What Training Will I need Flip-Flap Book

On-the-Job Training

College/University

Graduate School/ Advanced Degree

WHERE DID THESE PEOPLE GO TO COLLEGE?

OVERVIEW: Students will explore the educational path of some well-known celebrities. Then they can creatively make a display detailing what they have learned for a bulletin board or class book.

MATERIALS: Half sheets on page (61), construction paper, pencils, markers, photo of celebrity printed from the internet.

PROCEDURES:

1. Assign a celebrity to each student (or pair of students if they are working together).

2. Have student look at the information of "Where Did These People Go to College?" (pages 59-60).

3. Student can glue photo or draw picture of the celebrity (printed from the internet or hand drawn. in the framed part of figure 1 on page 61. The name of the celebrity should be written in the blank "Do you know that _____ ..."

4. Student should write information about the celebrity in the frame of figure 2 on page 61.

5. Create a foldable with the construction paper with figure 1 on outside and figure 2 on the inside so it opens like a book to show what type of training they had that can be displayed on a bulletin board or door decoration.

[REPRODUCIBLE]

WHERE DID THESE PEOPLE GO TO COLLEGE?

Below is a list of famous people and what college they went to.

NAME	JOB	COLLEGE ATTENDED	MAJOR/ STUDIED	MORE INFO
Alton Brown	Food Network Star	University of Georgia	Drama	Received a degree in drama from the University of Georgia and began his career in cinematography and film production.
Tom Brady	Football Player	University of Michigan	Organization Studies	
Ashton Kutcher	Actor	University of Iowa	Biochemical Engineering	He studied biochemical engineering with the hope of developing a cure for his brother's illness.
Oprah Winfrey	Actress/ TV Personality	Tennessee State University	Speech/ Drama	In college her focus was communication.
Michael Jordan	Basketball Player	University of North Carolina	Geography	Jordan left UNC early to enter the NBA, but eventually returned in to receive his degree.
Gordon Ramsay	Chef	N. Oxfordshire Technical College	Hotel Management	His early aptitude was in sports, but an injury changed his course on a culinary path.
Troy Aikman	Football Player	University of Oklahoma and UCLA	Sociology	Aikman promised his mom, when he left school for the NFL, that he would return and finish. At the age of 42, he finally fulfilled that commitment.
Natalie Portman	Actress	Harvard	A.B. degree Psychology.	In 2003, Portman graduated from Harvard College. Said, "I'd rather be smart than a movie star."

WHERE DID THESE PEOPLE GO TO COLLEGE?

Name	Job	College Attended	Major/ Studied	More Info
Barack Obama	President of the USA	Occidental, Columbia, and Harvard	Political Science	After 2 years at Occidental, he transferred to Columbia University. In 1988 he started graduate work at Harvard Law School.
JK Rowling	Author	Exeter	Classics	She also studied French and worked as a bilingual secretary after graduating college.
Peyton Manning	Football Player	Tennessee	Speech Communication	
Martin Luther King	Civil Rights Leader	Morehouse	Sociology	King continued his education at Crozer Theological Seminary and at Boston University's School of Theology, where he earned a doctorate in systemic theology,
Emeril	Chef	Johnson and Wales University	Culinary Arts	Started as a part-time job, baking bread in a Portuguese bakery.
Ann Hathaway	Actress	Vassar/NYU	English	

WHERE DID THESE PEOPLE GO TO COLLEGE
WORKSHEET

DID YOU KNOW THAT _____

FIGURE 1

DID YOU KNOW THAT _____

FIGURE 2

©YouthLight [61]

COMPARE AND CONTRAST

NAME: _____

DIRECTIONS: Compare and contrast college and your current level of school.

COLLEGE   _____ **SCHOOL**

Mahalia Mouse

OVERVIEW: In this lesson, students will be introduced to a mouse that gets stuck in a backpack of a college student and ends up taking courses at a university. There are several activities as well as a PowerPoint that can be used in conjunction with this lesson.

MATERIALS: *Mahalia Mouse Goes to College* by John Lithgow (also available on youtube.com at www.youtube.com/watch?v=A9TakQTqi-Q), PowerPoint that goes with it available on College Day CD, quiz-quiz-trade cards (on page 65), optional pennant worksheet on page (on page 66).

PROCEDURES:

1. Pre-teach Vocabulary (option, use PowerPoint on CD. See page 127 for overview of the PowerPoint that can be used to pre-teach the vocabulary).

2. Tell students that this is the story of a mouse who accidentally end ups at a college lecture while searching for food. The mouse becomes so excited about learning that she ends up going to school with the college students.

3. Ask students while listening to the story (or watching the video book at https://www.youtube.com/watch?v=A9TakQTqi-Q), to give a thumbs up each time they hear one of the words they learned.

4. After the story, review which words the students recognized.

5. Introduce Quiz-Quiz-Trade (see page 64).

OPTIONAL ACTIVITY:

The mouse did not think she could attend college and some of you might have reasons that you do not think you can either, but you CAN. There might be some obstacles that need to be overcome . . . but we are promoting a "you-can-do-it" mentality. Students will create a YOU CAN DO IT University Pennant (see page 66).

Quiz-Quiz-Trade College Style

OVERVIEW: This game allows students to review the material, while using a fun cooperative learning strategy.

MATERIALS: A set of questions printed or written out on cards (one card for each student), a bell (optional)

PROCEDURES:

1. Set clear expectations that this activity will stop immediately if there is any inappropriate behavior. Review the inappropriate behavior as: wandering around, refusing to take a question from a classmate, faces made at classmates if they do or don't know an answer, always going and/or waiting for a particular "friend," anything rude, anything that is not topic related.

2. Have two students come to the front of the room and model the following process:
   - Distribute the question cards so that each student has one.
   - Instruct students to find a partner.
   - Student 1 asks Student 2 the question written on the card and Student 2 answers.
   - Student 2 then asks Student 1 the question written on their card and Student 2 answers.

   - Student 1 and Student 2 trade cards.

3. Have a signal or bell to notify students when it is time to trade and find a new partner.

4. Typically, Quiz-Quiz-Trade lasts for about 10 minutes, but you could do it with more or less time depending on your time frame.

Option: Teacher/counselor can monitor by participating with a card. Most students love to ask adults the questions and it is a great way to model the activity.

[REPRODUCIBLE]

Quiz-Quiz-Trade Cards

Do you think you want to go to college? Why or why not?	**If you go to college, do you want to go close to where your family lives or far away? Why?**	**What might you want to be when you grow up? Do you think that will require a college degree?**
Having a major in college means that you are studying about one thing in particular. What is one thing you might want to major in? (Some examples are Science, Literature, Psychology, History)	**What do you think it would be like to live in a dorm room? This is a room where you and another person both live and share space.**	**Name a person you know who has gone to college. Do you know where they went?**
Do you think you would prefer big classes (called lectures) or smaller classes? Why?	**What do you think would be two difficult things about going to college?**	**Some people wait until they are older to go to college. Do you think you will want to go to college right after high school? Why or why not?**
Name two jobs that require a college degree.	**What is one way that students can get money to go to college?**	**How do you think college students manage to go to classes, study for tests, get enough sleep and still have fun?**
What kind of clubs or sports do colleges have that students can participate in?	**Which things should be most important to students in college: making new friends, learning interesting things, or cheering for sports teams? Why?**	**If you owned a business, would you want to hire people with a college degree?**

CREATE YOUR OWN COLLEGE PENNANT

NAME _____

DIRECTIONS: Create your own college pennant. Choose your college colors and draw in a mascot.

YOU CAN DO IT UNIVERSITY

WHAT IF I WASN'T ALLOWED TO GO TO SCHOOL?
THE BOY WHO HARNESSED THE WIND

OVERVIEW: Students will read a story about a child who isn't allowed to go to school. This activity will inspire students to think about what life would be like if they weren't allowed to go to school.

MATERIALS: Supplemental worksheets pages 68-69, *Boy Who Harnessed the Wind* by William Kamkwamba

PROCEDURES:

1. Discuss with the class that we are lucky to have schools that we can attend. Not only do we have the right to education, we are allowed to come to schools for free which is not true in all countries.

2. Read the *Boy Who Harnessed the Wind*.

3. Describe William's life and compare it to American teenagers and even your own.
   - What motivates people like William to attempt great things?
   - How would you describe William to someone who's never heard his story?
   - William wanted to go to school but couldn't because of money. Think about American students and how some people don't like coming to school. What do you think William would say to them?

EXTENSIONS:

Optional activity: Write questions on the parts of a pinwheel (available from many dollar stores). Pass the pinwheel around a circle and play an inspirational song. When you pause the song, the person with the pinwheel blows it and answers the question it lands on.

See William's blog for updates on the awesome things he is doing.
http://williamkamkwamba.typepad.com/

Writing Assignment: Imagine

NAME _____

Choose one of the following topics to write about:

— Imagine this world without schools. What would it be like?

— If I was told that I was not allowed to go to school. I would learn by...

_____

_____

_____

_____

_____

_____

_____

_____

_____

_____

_____

_____

_____

_____

_____

_____

_____

_____

_____

[REPRODUCIBLE]

WORKSHEET: BEING A MOTIVATED LIFELONG LEARNER

NAME _____

DIRECTIONS:

1. In each triangle of the windmill, write 3 goals for lifelong learning.

2. In the cloud, write a sentence describing how you can create the energy you will need to succeed.

3. In the scene, draw a picture representing you accomplishing one of your lifelong learning goals.

FUTURE DREAM CATCHERS

OVERVIEW: This is a great interactive lesson where students learn about goal setting and create a visual for these goals. This fantastic group craft will have a lasting visual impact to keep kids thinking.

MATERIALS: Hula Hoop (while in season they are available at some dollar stores), feathers copied on cardstock (see template page 74), plastic beads, hole puncher, 3 different color strips of paper, balls of yarn in a box, *Extra Yarn* by Mac Barnett

OPTIONAL:

1. Ask kids to come join you on the floor (or to stand up):
   - If they have dreams of being a professional athlete
   - If they have a goal of getting good grades this year
   - If they have hopes of going to college

2. Tell the class that you found a new book about hopes, dreams and possibilities that you wanted to share and read.

3. Read them *Extra Yarn*. (As you get to the part in the book where the archduke opens the box that he stole, have a box that you open towards you and act like it is empty.)

4. At the end of the story, review that the archduke was greedy and mean and when you are not kind, your future might be empty. But when you are kind and generous, your future possibilities are endless. Tell students that you hope that they are like the girl and that your box is always filled with . . . EXTRA YARN (simultaneously open the box toward the class so that they see that it is full of balls of yarn).

5. Show the class the partly-made Hula Hoop dream catcher (see image on page 71) and share that we will be making one of these for our class with the extra yarn.

6. Explain that students will soon get into pairs. Each pair will write down goals, dreams, and hopes on a paper feather and color it in. If they finish early, they can color the back of the feather.

7. Distribute one paper feather to every pair.

8. As students work, call them up one at a time and have them either weave the yarn in the center of the hoop (see page 71 for an example) or they can tie a bead to the yarn.

9. If time permits, students can tie their feathers to the hoop using the yarn adorned with beads (Please know that many times you might need to take these components to your office to assemble them.)

10. Tell students where these will be displayed (in their classroom, as a grade level displayed in the hall, etc.). See pages 72 and 73 for dream bubbles that can be displayed with dream catchers.

11. Leave students with the thought that dreams and hopes are wonderful, but ask them to think about the quote, "Goals are dreams with deadlines."

ALTERNATIVE PROJECTS INSTEAD OF GROUP DREAM CATCHER

I. Make "Individual Dream Catchers"

Materials: Paper Plates, Scissors, Markers/ Crayons, Yarn, Feathers, Beads, Hole Punch

1. Cut a hole in the center of the paper plate using the indentation as guide.

2. Punch 8-12 holes around the inside edge of the plate and tie a large string of yarn to one hole and create a web that crosses through the paper plate.

3. Decorate the outside of the paper plate with goals, wishes, and dreams.

4. Punch 3 holes to what will be the bottom of the plate. Tie yarn to a feather, string a few beads on the yarn and tie the yarn through each of the 3 holes.

II. See page 75 for Dream Catcher Worksheet

Sports

Family

COLLEGE

CAREER

 ©YouthLight

[REPRODUCIBLE]

MY DREAMCATCHER

A GOAL IS A DREAM WITH A DEADLINE.

MAKE DREAMS INTO A REALITY BY SETTING GOALS.

MY GOALS AND DREAMS:

_____

_____

_____

_____

_____

_____

_____

_____

_____

_____

_____

_____

_____

_____

_____

_____

_____

_____

_____

_____

_____

_____

COLLEGE APPLICATION

STUDENTS: Fill out this application to where you might like to go after high school (you can choose a four year college, an online program, the Armed Forces, or a vocational school).

MY COLLEGE APPLICATION

NAME _____

AGE _____ CURRENT GRADE LEVEL _____

PLACE WHERE I AM APPLYING _____

I THINK THAT I _____ HAVE GOOD ENOUGH GRADES TO COME HERE.

I THINK THAT I _____ HAVE GOOD ENOUGH BEHAVIOR TO COME HERE.

THE REASONS THAT I'LL BE A GOOD PART OF THIS COMMUNITY ARE

_____

_____

_____

_____

I THINK THAT ALWAYS LEARNING NEW THINGS _____

_____

_____

_____

_____

Get Your Hands On A Diploma

OVERVIEW: This craft activity is a fun way to introduce the idea that college is possible for all kids.

MATERIALS: Construction paper cut in half sheets in a variety of colors for hands, 9"x12" construction paper for background, white paper for diploma and string (or there are diploma shaped smarties).

PROCEDURES:

1. Ask students, "What is a diploma or degree?"

2. Review that a college degree says you have completed classes and learned skills from a particular college or university. Often you get a diploma (a piece of paper) to show what degree you have.

3. Say to students, "This activity will give you your first opportunity to put your hands on a diploma. Let's get started."

4. Distribute half-sheets of construction paper to students in the colors of their choice.

5. Have the students trace and cut out their hand.

6. Roll a sheet of white paper tightly, like a diploma, and tie it with string or yarn.

7. Ask the students to glue the hand (except for the thumb) to the upper left area of a sheet of black construction paper. The hand should be glued on with the thumb to the right. Leave the thumb unglued.

8. Explain to the children that the diploma symbolizes the key to their future. Place the rolled diploma across the hand and under the thumb on the sheet of paper.

LETTER TO THE ADMISSIONS OFFICE

DEAR ADMISSIONS OFFICE OF _____ ,

I would like to come to your school because _____
_____
_____
_____
_____ .

I would be a great student because _____
_____
_____
_____
_____ .

I know I will have to learn things like _____
_____
_____
_____
_____ .

It might be difficult for me to _____
_____
_____
_____
_____ .

but I will try my best. I look forward to _____
_____
_____
_____
_____ .

Sincerely,

[REPRODUCIBLE]

WRITING ABOUT MY FUTURE

I KNOW IT IS A LONG TIME AWAY, BUT WHEN I GET OUT OF HIGH SCHOOL I...

_____

_____

_____

_____

_____

_____

_____

_____

_____

_____

_____

_____

_____

_____

_____

_____

_____

_____

_____

BASIC COLLEGE VOCABULARY

NAME_____   **DATE**_____

DIRECTIONS: For each key word, write out the definition, use it in a sentence and draw a picture that represents this word.

KEY WORDS	DEFINITION	USE IT IN A SENTENCE	DRAW A PICTURE TO REPRESENT THE WORD
Scholarship			
Tuition			
Dormitory			
Campus			
Club Sports			
Course			
Major			

[REPRODUCIBLE]

What Will You Major In?

Name: _____

There are many things that you can choose to study in college. When you select the main thing you want to learn about in college, it is called your major.

Directions: Unscramble the words below to reveal some possible majors that college students choose.

1. cyoyslophg _____

2. shrytoi _____

3. oioylgb _____

4. auerrltiet _____

5. cuarnily _____ arts

6. simamttheac _____

7. eoaitdcun _____

8. hopyoisplh _____

9. syoocloig _____

10. nipsash _____

Clue box:

1. The science of understanding behavior.

2. Kind of like social studies.

3. The science of living things.

4. About books

5. Cooking

6. Addition and Subtraction

7. Teaching

8. Figuring out the meaning of life

9. Understanding people's social culture

10. A foreign language

PICTURE ME WITH A COLLEGE DEGREE

NAME _____

DIRECTIONS: You can either bring in a photo of yourself or draw a picture of yourself here.

PICTURE ME WITH A COLLEGE DEGREE.

[REPRODUCIBLE]

PICTURE ME WITH A COLLEGE DEGREE

NAME _____

DIRECTIONS: This page can be stapled beneath the previous page for a "lift and see" effect. On the lines, write some of your hopes for your future.

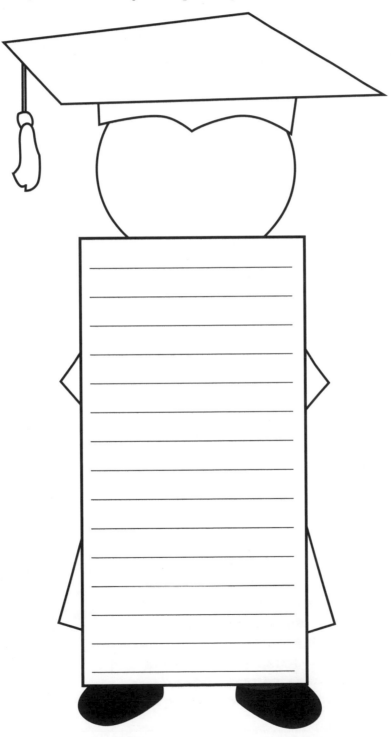

[REPRODUCIBLE]
QUOTES TO PONDER

DIRECTIONS: There a few ways to use these quote cards for a lesson. Distribute a card to each student or group of students. Allow them a short period of time to discuss what the quote means to them.

"I AM NOT WHAT HAS HAPPENED TO ME. I AM WHAT I CHOOSE TO BECOME." — CARL JUNG	"ONCE CHILDREN LEARN HOW TO LEARN, NOTHING IS GOING TO NARROW THEIR MIND. THE ESSENCE OF TEACHING IS TO MAKE LEARNING CONTAGIOUS, TO HAVE ONE IDEA SPARK ANOTHER." — MARVA COLLINS	"EDUCATION IS NOT THE FILLING OF A PAIL, BUT THE LIGHTING OF A FIRE." — WB YEATS
"THE ROOTS OF EDUCATION ARE BITTER, BUT THE FRUIT IS SWEET." — ARISTOTLE	"ARE YOUR EXCUSES MORE IMPORTANT THAN YOUR DREAMS?" — AUTHOR UNKNOWN	"YOU'RE OFF TO GREAT PLACES! TODAY IS YOUR DAY! YOUR MOUNTAIN IS WAITING, SO... GET ON YOUR WAY!" — DR. SEUSS
"AN EDUCATION ISN'T HOW MUCH YOU HAVE COMMITTED TO MEMORY, OR EVEN HOW MUCH YOU KNOW. IT'S BEING ABLE TO DIFFERENTIATE BETWEEN WHAT YOU KNOW AND WHAT YOU DON'T." — ANATOLE FRANCE	"INTELLIGENCE WITHOUT AMBITION IS A BIRD WITHOUT WINGS." — SALVADOR DALI	"GO CONFIDENTLY IN THE DIRECTION OF YOUR DREAMS. LIVE THE LIFE YOU HAVE IMAGINED." — THOREAU
"SHE TURNED HER CANT'S INTO CANS AND HER DREAMS INTO PLANS." — KOBI YAMADA	"WHEN DEFEAT COMES, ACCEPT IT AS A SIGNAL THAT YOUR PLANS ARE NOT SOUND, REBUILD THOSE PLANS, AND SET SAIL ONCE MORE TOWARD YOUR COVETED GOAL." — NAPOLEON HILL	"IN ONESELF LIES THE WHOLE WORLD AND IF YOU KNOW HOW TO LOOK AND LEARN, THE DOOR IS THERE AND THE KEY IS IN YOUR HAND." — J. KRISHNAMURTI

EDUCATION IS THE MOST POWERFUL WEAPON WHICH YOU CAN USE TO CHANGE THE WORLD.

NELSON MANDELA

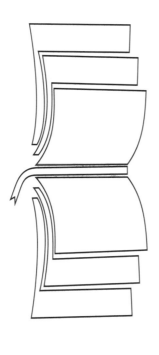

©YouthLight [85]

KIDS WITH THEIR
EYE ON THE FUTURE
DO BETTER IN
THE PRESENT.

AUTHOR UNKNOWN

IF YOU'RE NOT WILLING TO LEARN, NO ONE CAN HELP YOU. IF YOU'RE DETERMINED TO LEARN NO ONE CAN STOP YOU.

ZIG ZIGLAR

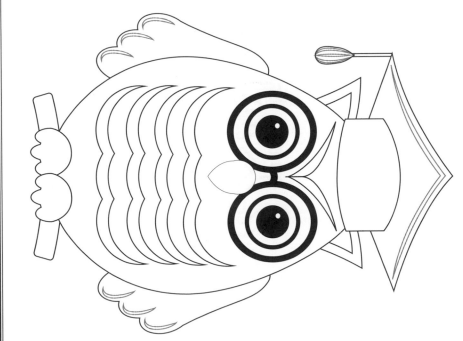

©YouthLight [87]

WHAT IF I FALL?

OH, BUT MY DARLING,
WHAT IF YOU FLY?

AUTHOR UNKNOWN

EDUCATION IS NOT THE FILLING OF A PAIL, BUT THE LIGHTING OF A FIRE.

W.B. YEATS

©YouthLight [89]

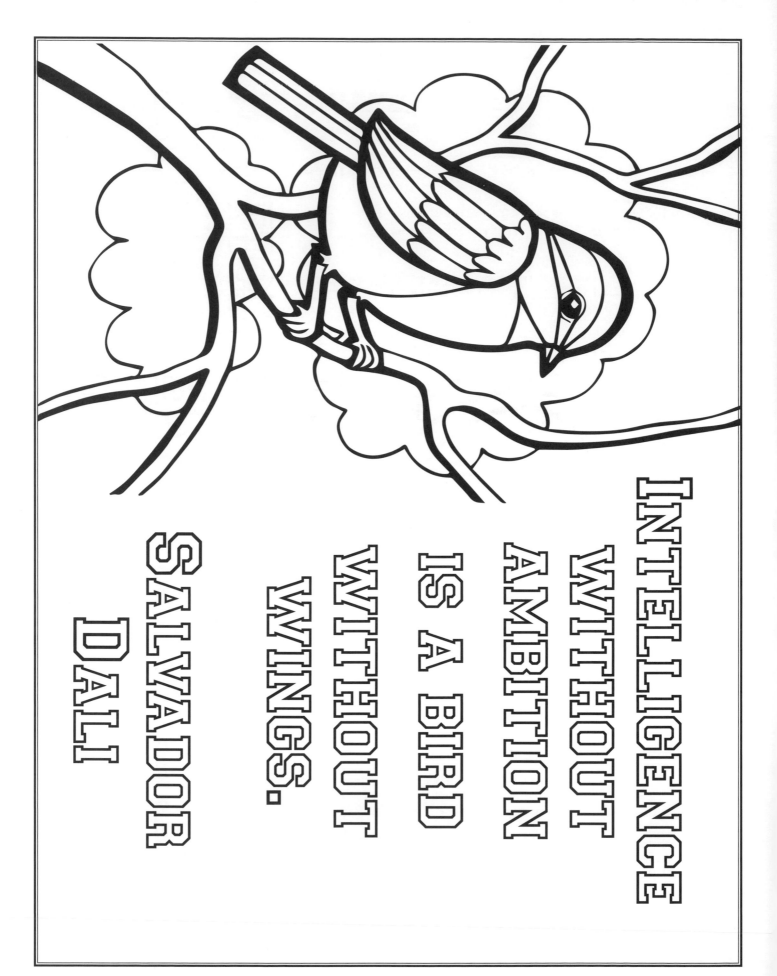

INTELLIGENCE
WITHOUT
AMBITION
IS A BIRD
WITHOUT
WINGS.

SALVADOR
DALI

 ©YouthLight

YOU'RE OFF TO GREAT PLACES!

TODAY IS YOUR DAY!

YOUR MOUNTAIN IS

WAITING. SO... GET

ON YOUR WAY!

DR. SEUSS

©YouthLight [91]

LET'S DO SOME MATH: HOW MUCH $$ CAN YOU MAKE?

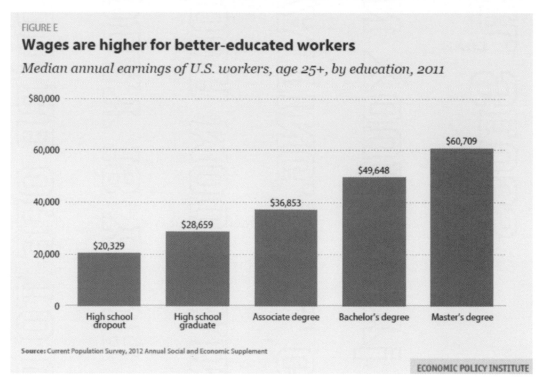

FIGURE E

Wages are higher for better-educated workers

Median annual earnings of U.S. workers, age 25+, by education, 2011

Source: Current Population Survey, 2012 Annual Social and Economic Supplement

ECONOMIC POLICY INSTITUTE

Above is a graph that shows the average of how much a person made in 2011 according to how much education they had. Look at the graph to answer the questions below.

1. How much might someone make each year if they got a job after earning a four year college degree?

2. How much more money would a person make if they finished high school, compared to if they dropped out of high school?

3. Create your own graph using the average annual salary rounded to the nearest 10,000. (For example, high school dropouts would round to 20,000, a 4-year college graduate would round to $50,000, etc.)

How Can You Pay for College?

1. _____ **Loan**

     a. money that someone borrows from a bank with the understanding that it will be paid back over time

2. _____ **Tuition**

     b. a student can apply for this which provides money based on the student's need of help

3. _____ **Scholarship**

     c. money given to support a student's education, awarded for academic or other achievement

4. _____ **Financial Aid**

     d. money paid for where you live and what you eat

5. _____ **Room and Board**

     e. money that is paid for classes

©YouthLight [93]

BEING A LIFELONG DETECTIVE

DIRECTIONS: Look at the clues in your life and after answering the following questions, think about what your lifelong learning might look like.

Do you hope to go to college? _____

Do you want to try new hobbies when you get older? _____

Do you know any adults who like to learn new things? Explain. _____

_____

_____

_____

_____

_____

At what age do you think people stop learning? Explain. _____

_____

_____

_____

_____

Commit yourself to lifelong learning. The most valuable asset you'll ever have is your mind and what you put into it.
– Brian Tracy

[**REPRODUCIBLE**]

COMIC STRIP – MY FUTURE

NAME: _____

DIRECTIONS: Draw a comic strip of your future with drawings and speech bubbles.

HERE IS THE STORY ON THE LIFE LONG LEARNING I WILL DO.

©YouthLight [95]

BINGO FOR COLLEGE LINGO

DIRECTIONS: Put one of following words in each block. You can put the words more than once, but make sure it is under a different letter. Then we will play College Lingo Bingo.

G	R	A	D

DORMITORY	TUITION	SCHOLARSHIP	COURSE
PROFESSOR	GRADUATE	DEGREE	GPA

Time Management

MATERIALS: Different size paper plates with the different daily tasks written on them (i.e.; study, sleep, go to classes, work out, eat, go to movies) magnets, white board, clean room, hang out with friends, talk on phone to parents, do assignments, surf the internet, play video games, have part-time job)

PROCEDURES:

1. Read one of the articles (pages 101 or 102) about a real college experience, then do this activity about time management and how it is often one of the challenges of college life.

2. Show class the back of the paper plates and tell them that these are all of the activities that a college student wants to do in a week. Have them guess what might be on the plates. Large plates are for large tasks, smaller plates for smaller tasks.

3. Draw a large box on a magnetic white board and tell students that the box represents one week. How can you fit all of the plates in the box?

4. Allow student volunteer to come up and try and decide what is most important. Using the magnets, have them place the plates inside the box. See what is left out.

5. Discuss the concept of prioritizing and putting the important things first.

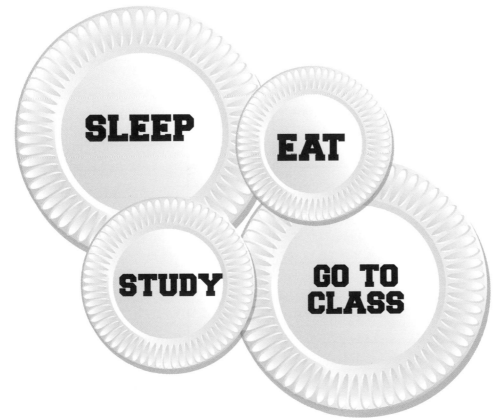

Social Media Profile Page

Name: _____

School: _____

Location: _____

Teacher: _____

Grade: ___

Birthday: _____ **Age:** _____

PHOTO/PICTURE HERE

Status Update: _____

Groups You belong to:

_____
_____
_____
_____
_____
_____

Goals and Dreams:

_____
_____
_____
_____
_____
_____
_____
_____

Friend's Comments About You:	
DATE	COMMENT

SNAPSHOT OF MY FUTURE

NAME:_____

WHAT TYPE OF JOB WILL I HAVE?

WHAT TYPE OF TRAINING WILL I NEED?

WHAT ELSE WILL BE IN MY FUTURE?

©YouthLight [99]

COLLEGE READINESS ARTICLES

The following pages contain articles written on different perspectives of post high school life. These can be used in several ways.

- Divide the class in small groups. Give one of the articles to each group. Have the small groups read the article, answer the question(s) and then present a summary to the large group.

- Divide the class in small groups. Give one of the articles to each group. Have the small groups read the article, answer the question(s) and then switch articles with another group. Continue to switch articles until time is up.

- Present a short synopsis of the articles (or the titles) and have each student choose the article that they think sounds most interesting. Then, they can find a partner to share what they learned.

- Distribute an article to each student randomly. After a certain amount of time (5-10 minutes), have students get into groups and discuss the article and make a poster summarizing the topic.

UNIVERSITY

INVEST IN YOUR FUTURE

 ©YouthLight

ARTICLE 1

WHAT WOULD A COLLEGE ADMISSIONS DIRECTOR TELL YOU?

Dave Graves is the Senior Associate Director of Admissions at the University of Georgia. His job includes reading applications, and helping decide which students will be admitted to this college.

Q: What advice would you give to young students who one day hopes to go to college?

A: The best thing a student right now can do is work hard in the classroom and put academics first. And my favorite is to read, read, read. It will boost their vocabulary, strengthen their communication skills, help them be creative, and prepare them for college.

Q: What are the most important things you look for when you are deciding what students get in to the University of Georgia?

A: The most important things are taking challenging classes and doing well in them. We look at test scores and other things, but how a student does in challenging high school classes shows us a lot about how a student might do in college.

Q: What if a student doesn't think that they will be able to have enough money to pay for college?

A: A student and their family should look at the cost of a college before applying, but often there is a chance for financial help for families who need it (grant money, loans, scholarships, etc.). Also, if a student is a great student, they might be able to receive scholarships based on their academics from the college.

Q: Are students' hobbies and interests looked at when you decide who gets into UGA?

A: We do look beyond the academic grades, although that is the most important factor we consider. We also look at clubs, sports, activities and leadership qualities.

QUESTION:

What are some important things that colleges look for when you apply to go there?

_____

_____

_____

_____

_____

[REPRODUCIBLE]

ARTICLE 2
GOING TO COLLEGE FAR FROM HOME

Joanna and Maddy Spencer grew up in White Plains, NY. They both go to college far away from home, and they both are very involved in many activities on their college campuses. Joanna Spencer is a senior at Northwestern University in Chicago, Illinois. Madeline is a sophomore at Vanderbilt University in Nashville, Tennessee.

JOANNA

MADDY

DESCRIBE HOW IT IS TO BE AT COLLEGE FAR FROM HOME.

Joanna: I like it. It's definitely not for everyone, but I like being able to have this experience. How many other times in your life are you really able to choose to live in any place you want?	**Maddy:** It's good and bad. I definitely feel more independent being far from home. There was only one time when I was very sick and really wanted to be near home so my family could take care of me, but I have a good support system of friends who were there for me.

WHAT ADVICE DO WISH YOU HAD WHEN LOOKING AT WHERE TO GO TO COLLEGE?

Joanna: To tell my parents that this was a decision that I had to make for myself, and their opinions are helpful, but they cannot make the choice for me.	**Maddy:** Go where you think you'll be happy. If you need to be closer to home because you need family support to take care of yourself, that's fine. Go with your gut on what school is the best fit for you.

WHAT HAVE BEEN SOME INTERESTING CLASSES YOU HAVE TAKEN?

Joanna: I've taken a bunch of good classes, and a bunch of bad ones. I think that the best classes are a combination of interesting material and awesome professors.	**Maddy:** I really enjoyed a class called applied behavioral sciences. It was so much fun. We took a personality test and realized how it applied to jobs and the real world.

WHAT THINGS ON CAMPUS ARE YOU INVOLVED IN AND WHICH ONE HAS IMPACTED YOU MOST?

Joanna: 1. Living on campus freshman year in a big dorm. 2. Marching band!!!! ohmygosh marching band (it's like a fraternity that you are automatically allowed to be in). 3. Taekwondo – a continuation of my sports interests before college.	**Maddy:** I am most involved in the rowing team and my sorority. Rowing has definitely impacted me the most. It has taught me not only how to eat and stay fit but how to carry myself, how to respect my teammates even if I don't like them.

QUESTIONS:

1. Would you want to go to college close to home or far away? Why?
2. Joanna and Maddy are very involved in activities on their college campuses. What activities would you want to participate in at college?

ARTICLE 3
BACK TO SCHOOL AS AN ADULT

Some people go to college right after high school and some people wait to go until they are a bit older. Lucretia Elliot got married and had 3 kids before she decided that she wanted to pursue a college degree. Read below to find out more about her.

Q: What inspired you to go back for your degree?

A: My kids and the urge to learn inspired me to go back to school.

Q: What is the biggest challenge?

A: The biggest challenge is finding time to do my homework/study in the midst of work, kids, and sports.

Q: What is your favorite part of being a college student?

A: My favorite part of being a college student is observing other students that are MUCH younger than me! It is amazing how smart and creative they are. Their technology skills are absolutely amazing!

Q: What advantage do you have over younger students?

A: Honestly, the fact that I have a family and "real" responsibilities.... I have no time to party, sleep in late, etc. I understand that I am paying for my classes and therefore, I MUST do well to benefit!

Q: Advice for students deciding if they should go to college right out of high school.

A: DO IT!!! The longer you wait, the harder it will be. Take advantage of being young and having fun, WHILE you get an education. College is a great time to meet new people and discover yourself!

QUESTIONS:

1. Do you think you will want to go to college right after high school? Why or why not?

2. What are some reasons that going to college when you are older make it more difficult?

3. What are some reasons older students take college more seriously?

ARTICLE 4

THE ARMED FORCES OPTION

Major Sam Allen enlisted in the Armed Forces after his sophomore year at the University of Kentucky to pay for his college education. He was commissioned as an officer in 2002 and currently serves as the Field Artillery Planner for the Brigade Commander. Major Allen is in charge of training all Fire Support Officers in the Brigade. Additionally, he is responsible for planning special projects such as community outreach, staff training, and equipment management.

WHAT ARE SOME OTHER REASONS THAT PEOPLE ENLIST IN THE ARMED FORCES?

People join the Army for a number of reasons. For some, it is the only way to escape life as they know it. It is an opportunity to prove to themselves or others that they can be better. For others, it is a stepping stone to college or another career field. And there are those who do have truly patriotic motivations.

HOW HAS THE ARMED FORCES SUPPORTED YOUR EDUCATION?

The Army reduced my student loan debt significantly. Additionally, they fully funded my graduate degree program and allowed me to take 18 months to complete it while on active duty. My graduate degree is in National Security Affairs.

WHAT ADVICE DO YOU HAVE FOR THOSE WHO ARE THINKING ABOUT CONSIDERING THE ARMED FORCES AS THEIR POST HIGH SCHOOL PATH?

It is an excellent opportunity that will allow you to pursue any number of paths. If anything, it allows a young person to spend three to five years developing themselves mentally and physically while they figure out their own path. It is truly a fulfilling career.

QUESTION:

What are some reasons that people join the armed forces?

[REPRODUCIBLE]

ARTICLE 5

THE LIFE OF A CHEF

Read this interview from Chef Jeff McGar who has been a chef for over 25 years.

WHAT INSPIRED YOU TO BECOME A CHEF?

My love for cooking. I've been cooking professionally since I was 16. But before then, I started cooking in my Mom's kitchen at age 10. I enjoy the rush of being really busy and having multiple tasks to complete in a short amount of time. As I progressed in my career, I started to enjoy and appreciate the art of the culinary sciences.

DID YOU SEEK A COLLEGE DEGREE AND/OR GO TO CULINARY SCHOOL?

By the time I realized that is what I wanted to do professionally, I was already too far advanced in the restaurant industry. Meaning I had worked my way into the General Manager Position but still fell back to the "back of house" cooking as much as possible. So I went through the American Culinary Federation's apprenticeship program and learned the art of cooking as an apprentice under a certified master chef and at a five star certified Country Club.

WHAT ARE THE ADVANTAGES TO GETTING FORMAL TRAINING VS. ON-THE-JOB TRAINING?

I think it's the other way around. I think on-the-job training is more valuable because you are hands on and you learn your craft in a practical situation. After 3 years I was promoted to Sous Chef and became the supervisor over kids that were coming out of culinary school. At the end of my apprenticeship program, I felt that I was more well-rounded learning the culinary skills, restaurant management, and overall experience needed to run a restaurant. Those are skills that cannot be taught in a classroom setting. I was paid to learn my craft rather than having a $70,000 loan to pay off.

WHAT ADVICE DO YOU HAVE FOR STUDENTS DECIDING IF THEY SHOULD GO TO COLLEGE OR VOCATIONAL SCHOOL AFTER HIGH SCHOOL?

I think that everyone needs to do what's right for them. It depends on the person and their learning style and motivation. Being a chef is very hard work and you have to be prepared to work HARD. You need to set short and long term goals and set a course to obtain your goals.

ARTICLE 6

FIRST ONE IN MY FAMILY TO GO TO COLLEGE

Hilda Queiroz is the first one in her family to go to college. She was born in Brazil, grew up in Marietta, GA and attends Mississippi State University. Learn more about this young woman who has a drive for success and has achieved her dreams with hard work and has a bright future ahead.

Q: WHEN DO YOU FIRST REMEMBER WANTING TO GO TO COLLEGE?

A: I don't really remember wanting or not wanting to go to college. My parents just made it clear that I was going to college so I better work hard in school. That's all there really was to it.

Q: WHY WAS IT IMPORTANT TO YOUR PARENTS THAT YOU WENT TO COLLEGE?

A: My parents wanted better for their children and they knew that education was key for that. My mom made a deal with me very early that if I did my part in school, she would find a way to pay for school. Sometimes I'd comment on something particularly nice and my dad would remind me that if I worked hard and went to college, it could be mine. They had a vision of a better future for us and that's why me going to college was so important to them.

Q: HOW DID YOU LOOK INTO SCHOLARSHIPS AND WHAT ADVICE DO YOU HAVE ABOUT THIS PROCESS?

A: I started looking at scholarships online on my own and I felt a little lost so I went to my high school counselor and she was determined to help. I also reached out to other students who were the first in their family to go to college and asked about their experiences and advice. My most important tool in searching for scholarships was my high school counselor who really committed herself to helping me. My advice is not to get discouraged even though the process can be so overwhelming. Keep searching because there are so many scholarships out there.

Q: WHAT ARE THE EXPECTATIONS IN KEEPING SCHOLARSHIPS?

A: It depends on the scholarship. My largest scholarship requires me to keep my GPA above a 3.0. Another one requires that my portfolio grow every year to exhibit leadership and growth. Another one requested that I send out thank you cards to the family that sponsored the scholarship. All of them have different requirements but good grades are the basis for all of them.

 ©YouthLight

Q: WHAT IS YOUR FAVORITE PART ABOUT COLLEGE?

A: I like the freedom to do or be whatever I want. With so many different people, there's a place for everyone. As I finish up my senior year, I think one of my favorite things though is taking classes that actually pertain to exactly what I want to do. It's awesome to take classes that are interesting and useful versus lecture classes where you're 1 of 250 and teachers don't know you exist. In my small classes the teachers and students are on a first name basis.

Q: WHAT IS THE MOST CHALLENGING THING ABOUT COLLEGE?

A: Balancing everything is tough. There are so many different things to get involved in so balancing school, work and extracurricular activities can sometimes be really hard. It sometimes feels like there aren't enough hours in the day to get everything done.

QUESTIONS:

1. What qualities does Hilda have that have enabled her to go to college? Do you have those qualities?

2. How can students find out about scholarships and what do students need to do to keep the scholarships?

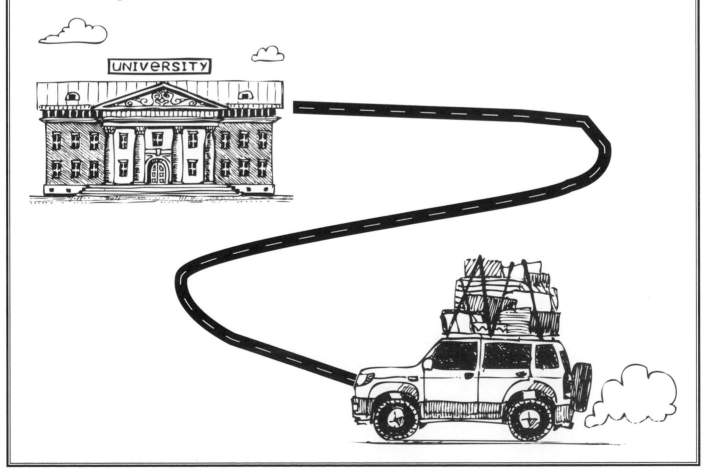

[REPRODUCIBLE]

ARTICLE 7

TRADE SCHOOL/VOCATIONAL TRAINING

Dennis Karpinski is an electrician and has been his own boss for over 15 years. He works hard and still has to continue his education so he can stay up-to-date on codes and current technology.

WHAT KIND OF TRAINING DO YOU NEED TO BE AN ELECTRICIAN? DISCUSS INITIAL TRAINING AND ALSO IF YOU HAVE TO CONTINUE TRAINING TO STAY UP-TO-DATE.

There are different requirements in each state. In the state of Georgia, you need 4 years of experience and pass an 8 hour test to be licensed. I have to take extra classes each year, called continuing education to keep up-to-date on code changes. People want to hire someone who knows what they're doing, so it is important to get training to be an expert at what you do.

YOU ARE YOUR OWN BOSS. WHAT ARE THE BENEFITS TO THIS?

There are good things and difficult things about being your own boss. On the positive side, it is possible to make more money being my own boss and I can pick the people I want to do jobs for. I also set my own hours of work.

WHAT KIND OF CHARACTER TRAITS DO YOU HAVE TO SHOW ON THE JOB?

I have to know how to get along with people and really be a good listener. I also need to be respectful of the client's home and work neatly. To be good at anything, you need to know your job. One of the things I learned with experience is to be able to look at what someone is asking me to do and be able to estimate how much work will go into the job and how to price.

IF A YOUNG PERSON WANTS TO BE AN ELECTRICIAN, WHAT ADVICE WOULD YOU HAVE FOR THEM?

Even though some states don't require going to a trade school (also called vocational school), it would be helpful to learn the trade and know how to run a business.

DISCUSSION QUESTIONS:

1. Are there requirements for electricians to be licensed?

2. What are some important character traits for an electrician (or anyone on the job) to show?

DOOR DECORATIONS AND BULLETIN BOARDS

One of the ideas to implement for College Day is to have teachers/classes decorate their doors. This gives an opportunity for the classes to go on a "Tour of Doors." While teachers are inherently creative, the following ideas of door decorations have templates to go along with them so they would be easy to replicate. Each of these ideas could nicely supplement a lesson from Chapter 2 as well.

CONTENTS

THE FUTURE'S SO BRIGHT

DIRECTIONS: Have the students color the rims of their sunglasses and label what they see in their future on the lenses of the glasses. They can then draw a self-portrait on separate paper and glue the sunglasses over the eyes.

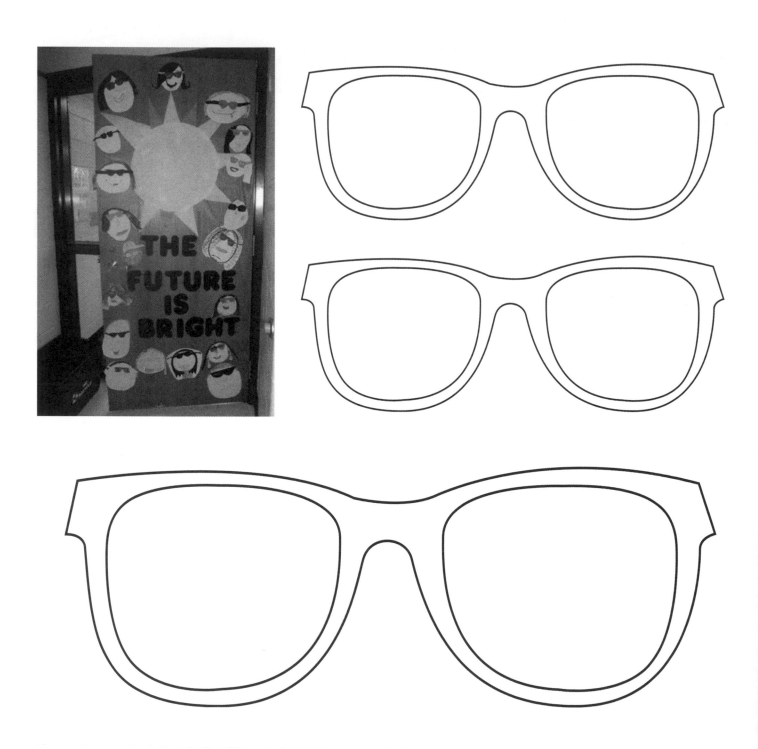

FOLLOW YOUR YELLOW BRICK ROAD

DIRECTIONS: Students can either draw their picture or glue a photo of themselves in the face of the dog, scarecrow, lion, tinman, or person who is on the yellow brick road. Students can then decorate the building as the place of higher learning/training that they see themselves going to. A bulletin board or door decoration can be created by putting the characters on a yellow road and have the places of learning towards the end of the road.

©YouthLight [113]

SETTING THE STAGE FOR LIFE

DIRECTIONS: Students can decorate a ticket, a star or a director's clapboard for this door decoration idea.

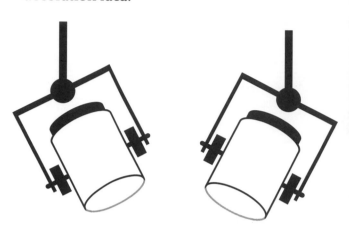

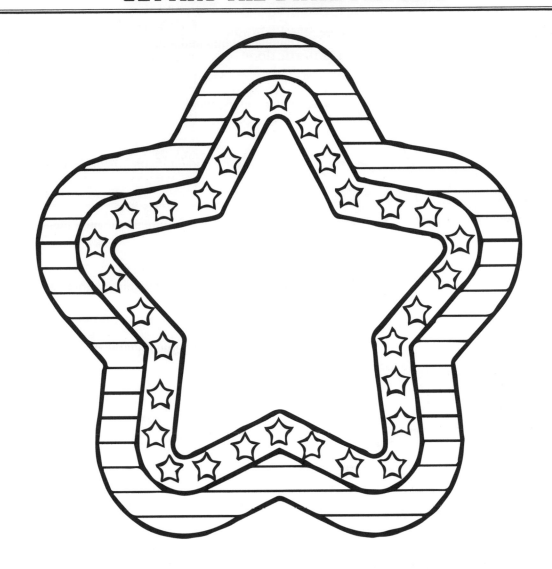

Admit One

Admit One

OUR EYES ARE ON THE FUTURE

DIRECTIONS: Students can write in the eyeballs the hopes they have for the future. This would make a fantastic door decoration.

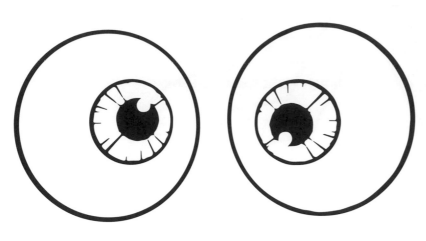

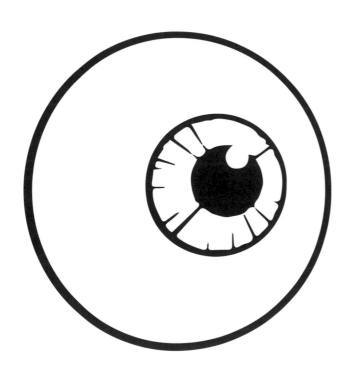

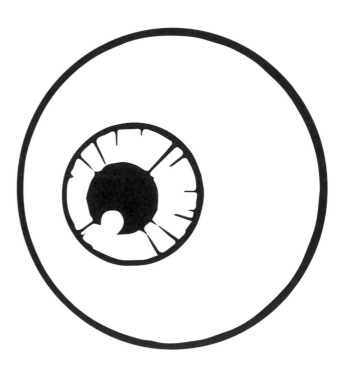

LET'S CHAT ABOUT MY FUTURE

DIRECTIONS: Copy these templates of text conversations and allow the students to fill in the conversation. Another option is to white out the question and make up your own. Let the students finish the conversation and then post them in a display, bulletin board, or door decoration.

WHAT'S ON THE LINE IN THE FUTURE?
OR
MY FUTURE LOOKS T-RIFFIC!

DIRECTIONS: Students can decorate these t-shirts with the logo/mascot of their favorite college, or they can write out some ideas for the future with words that represent their hopes and dreams.

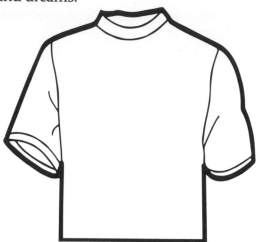

KEEP CALM AND GRADUATE

DIRECTIONS: This template can be used to create a bulletin board like "Keep Calm and Graduate". Each child can decorate a graduation cap or just one can be used.

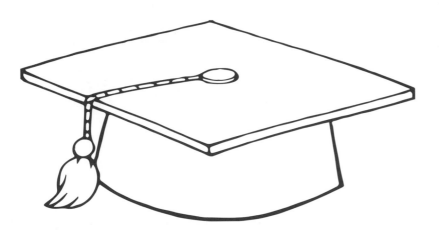

©YouthLight [119]

WHOooo is going to College?

DIRECTIONS: Students can decorate an owl with their personal goals.

COLLEGE BOUND KIDS POPPING UP

DIRECTIONS: Use the following pages to create this bulletin board. Students can each decorate a piece of popcorn with their college or future dreams.

CHOOSE THE SCHOOL THAT FITS YOU

DIRECTIONS: Students can decorate a puzzle piece with their personal goals.

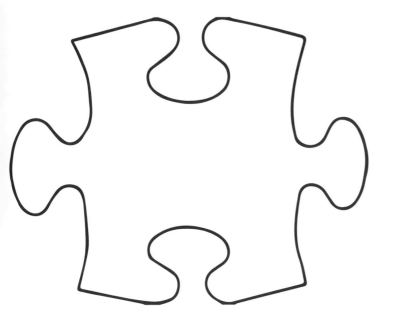

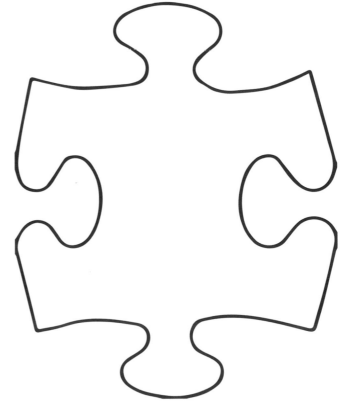

CLASS OF _____

Students can create the pennant of their choice for their post high school aspirations.

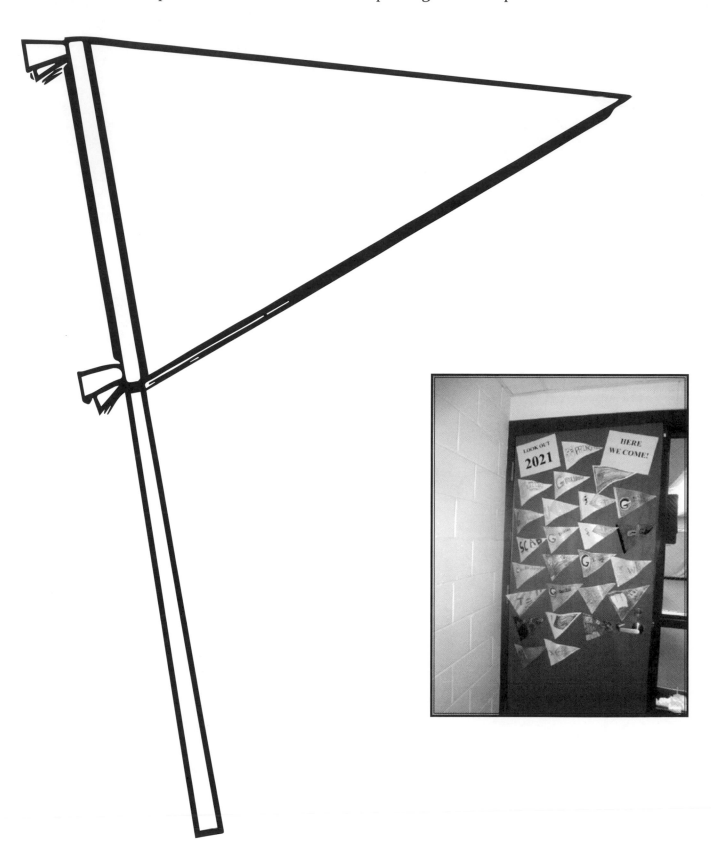

UNLOCK YOUR POTENTIAL

RECIPE FOR SUCCESS

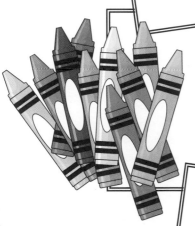

FROM CRAYONS TO COLLEGE

S___CCESS IS ONLY POSSIBLE WITH YOU!

POWERPOINT PRESENTATION OVERVIEWS

POWERPOINT A: FRAMEWORK FOR A CLASS LESSON

(See the CD for the PowerPoint presentation)

This PowerPoint can be a framework for a classroom lesson. It is a great ready-made base or supplement to any of the lessons in Chapter 2. This PowerPoint allows students to guess the vocabulary word for the picture and animates the words in afterwards. Additionally, the PowerPoint gives a brief overview of what College Day will look like and addresses some of concerns students might have about college like, "Am I smart enough?" One of the slides addresses the opportunity to potentially make more money with higher degrees. This PowerPoint provides many opportunities for discussion.

POWERPOINT B: PRESENTATION FOR ADMINISTRATORS/ADVISORY COUNCIL/ STAKEHOLDERS

(See the CD for the PowerPoint presentation)

This PowerPoint will help you present to your stakeholders (whether that be an Advisory Council or Administrators). The PowerPoint gives an overview of why college readiness is important for younger students and how it can be implemented. There is also a slide that shows data that can be collected showing positive results in how student perception can be changed through implementing a College Day.

ABOUT THE AUTHOR

Lisa King is a school counselor in Marietta, GA where she has had the pleasure of being an elementary school counselor for 17 years (and counting) at the same school. She has received numerous awards in her county and presented her programs to counselors throughout the US. She enjoys creating new lessons that help students and inspire counselors. She lives in Marietta,GA with her husband and daughter.